PURE MOXIE

Pure Moxie

A Memoir

Leda Sanford

iUniverse, Inc.
New York Bloomington

Pure Moxie
A Memoir

Editing *Jessica Mullins and Steve Boga*
Consulting *Leslie Keenan and Tema Goodwin*
Cover Photo *Robert Sanford*
Special Thanks *Sharon Jones*

— "When Everything Changed: The Amazing Journey of American Women from 1960 to present," *by Gail Collins, © 2009, Little, Brown and Company.*

iUniverse books may be ordered through booksellers or by contacting:

iUniverse
1663 Liberty Drive
Bloomington, IN 47403
www.iuniverse.com
1-800-Authors (1-800-288-4677)

Because of the dynamic nature of the Internet, any Web addresses or links contained in this book may have changed since publication and may no longer be valid.

ISBN: 978-1-4502-5586-8 (sc)
ISBN: 978-1-4502-5587-5 (dj)
ISBN: 978-1-4502-5588-2 (ebk)

Library of Congress Control Number: 2010913325

Printed in the United States of America

iUniverse rev. date: 9/29/2010

Dedicated to Betty Friedan

CONTENTS

PREFACE

In March of 1970 about one hundred women took over the office of John Mack Carter, the publisher and editor of *Ladies' Home Journal*. At his side during the long day of confrontation was Lenore Hershey, the only woman in management, who demanded to know how many of "you girls" were married. The protestors unveiled a long list of demands, including free day care for all employees, no more "advertisements that degrade women," and an end to the popular "Can This Marriage Be Saved?" column. The protestors also wanted to eliminate all celebrity articles, "all articles oriented toward the preservation of youth," and "slanted romantic stories glorifying women's traditional role"—a litany that pretty much did away with the entire table of contents.

—*When Everything Changed: The Amazing Journey of American Women from 1960 to the Present*, by Gail Collins

In 1975, one woman was selected to take over American Home Publishing, a branch of Downe Communications, which owned *Ladies' Home Journal*. John Mack Carter had acquired American Home Publishing with hopes of promoting the values he held dear—epitomized by American colonial furniture and a traditional lifestyle. His dream was not realized.

When Carter left and joined the Hearst Corporation, I was named president, publisher, and editor-in-chief of American Home Publishing. I was instructed to reposition *American Home* magazine. It was a final effort to save the ailing publication.

1. Breaking the Glass Ceiling

Swaying slightly from side to side in my first executive armchair with the backdrop of Manhattan visible through my corner office windows, I leaned over the *New York Times*, which was spread open on my desk, and reread Phil Dougherty's advertising column:

"Leda Sanford Named President and Publisher of *American Home*."

I felt thrilled, proud, and scared. I wasn't prepared for this challenge.

Dougherty's column kicked off the start of each new day for most publishing and advertising executives in the seventies. It was read at the breakfast table and on trains and buses that brought them to Manhattan. For many, "Did you see Dougherty's column today?" was part of the opening greeting.

Today's column, with my name in the headline, would create a buzz. It would confirm rumors that had been circulating for weeks and prompt this question: Who is Leda Sanford?

It had all happened so quickly and in such an unorthodox way. Five years earlier, I had been a bored housewife in suburban Westchester. Now here I was on the fourth floor of the Downe Building, sitting in an oversized executive leather chair behind an equally oversized walnut desk, which I had inherited from John Mack Carter, the former occupant. Through the angled windows, I could see down Lexington Avenue. I swiveled away from the paneled office and looked across Fifty-first Street to the Hudson River.

I swiveled to the left to contemplate the sideboard with its silver coffee service. I'd learned earlier that morning that the coffee service would be maintained by Mabel, the staff maid, who also ran the *American Home* kitchen where the magazine's recipes were tested.

This was 1975, and publishers were treated like princes, with all the accoutrements of a royal lifestyle. I had inherited two secretaries and my own private bathroom. John Mack Carter had also maintained a car and driver, who was even now parked down front, waiting for me. This was not where I had expected to be when I'd met with John Mack Carter, the guru of women's magazines, in his new headquarters at *Good Housekeeping* magazine in the Hearst Building.

Staring out of the window, I sipped my coffee and thought back to three months before.

After two years at *Men's Wear* magazine, I was bored with trade journalism and eager for a new challenge, although working as the publication's editor had been an enlightening whirlwind. I had landed that job via a meeting with *Men's Wear* publisher Mort Gordon after working as editor of *Teens & Boys* magazine (my first job in the industry) for three and a half years. My friend Allen Boorstein, president of the Rob Roy Company, warned me that although he was married, Mort was a ladies' man.

"Promise you won't fall in love with him, and I'll get you a meeting," Allen said.

"I promise."

I lied, knowing I was already infatuated with Mort—I had seen him at a few industry functions.

Mort was tall, with a strong, classic Greek profile (although he was Jewish) and a beautiful head of wavy gray hair. When he was formally dressed in a tuxedo and black tie, he fit my fantasy of a classic 1940s' movie star. His reputation as a womanizer with a great sense of humor made him a hero to most of the men he dealt with. The bond between us was forged while I worked for him at *Men's Wear* and when my need for men was at its peak. It was the beginning of an on-again, off-again relationship that spanned decades.

But as time at *Men's Wear* passed, I felt uncomfortable with the growing number of people who suspected Mort and I were having an affair.

And I was tired of the celebrity focus that dominated women's magazines (and still does after fifty years): the boring, copycat graphics that made one issue indistinguishable from another; the constant parade of movie stars, inappropriate role models for trapped housewives.

I was ready to move on.

Through a friend, I obtained an appointment with John Mack Carter, presenting myself as a candidate for his editorial team. I thought *Good Housekeeping* could use a face-lift and had the temerity to tell Carter that the very term "good housekeeping" would soon become irrelevant. (More than thirty-five years later it still exists.) Carter listened as I passionately described my vision of a magazine for the new American woman, one that would help her juggle her myriad demands in this new world. One of my themes was simplicity, finding ways to simplify life rather than complicate it with high-maintenance décor and time-consuming recipes.

Since John Mack Carter, a devotee of the Colonial lifestyle, had imprinted that concept on the magazine, he seemed leery. It didn't stop me.

"John, women today are trying to redefine themselves. They need help coping with the demands of homemaking and the guilt that comes from their inability to meet unrealistic standards at home. They need permission to do less housework and invest more in their personal fulfillment."

I related to these women. I had been suffocating in the suburban life I had fled.

Carter, who had been forced to sell *American Home*, teetering on the brink of bankruptcy, to the Charter Company, was intrigued with my ideas. Perhaps it was the fire in my speech, perhaps it was the words I chose to paint a picture of who the *new* American woman might be that prompted him to lean back in his chair, tap his pipe, and declare, "You're an editorial animal."

He was right. To this day, I have a visceral response to the marriage of words and pictures in print.

With that, he referred me to Jacqueline Brandywine, a consultant to the Charter Company who had been hired to screen candidates for the new management team at *American Home*.

We met in her office at Rockefeller Center. She was an attractive brunette, spilling over with self-confidence, New York style. Elegantly dressed and coifed, she deliberately spread out copies of recent issues of *American Home*. She paraded back and forth behind her desk, pointing at the covers, stopping to flip pages and shake her head. "Uh oh ... no, no ... this must change."

"Do you agree the only hope for this magazine is repositioning?" she asked.

"I agree. That's why I'm here."

"Good. Look at *Cosmopolitan*."

She touted *Cosmopolitan* as an example of a successful turnaround and lauded Helen Gurley Brown as the architect of this success story. *Cosmo* was a magazine that had identified the newly liberated woman, with the help of Brown's best-selling book, *Sex and the Single Woman*. Brandywine believed that only similar radical surgery would save this patient, though she recognized that repositioning a magazine was one of the most dangerous maneuvers in the business. Nevertheless, she directed me, challenged me, to develop an editorial plan for repositioning *American Home*. She wanted a table of contents, a graphic philosophy, and a reader profile. Charter wanted to launch the new look by January 1976. We had eight months. (I never knew if there had been any other applicants for this position.)

Within a week, I delivered my outline for the new *American Home*. It consisted of a total revision of the editorial content. We would head in a more modern direction, away from the American colonial emphasis and the Campbell Soup casseroles, emphasizing, for example, interior decoration for easy maintenance and recipes that stimulated the imagination as well as the appetite. The new *American Home* would appeal to a new kind of woman, someone who was looking for practical solutions to the challenge of home management without abdicating her responsibilities.

"This won't be our mother's magazine anymore," I said as I made my presentation to Brandywine.

She liked my plan, and a few days later I received a call from Raymond K. Mason's secretary, asking when I would be available to meet with Mason. I had no idea who he was until, while waiting in the reception area, I perused the company's annual report. He was the chairman of the Charter Company, a Jacksonville, Florida–based oil conglomerate.

As I walked into his austere and sparsely furnished office on the fourth floor of the Downe building on the corner of Lexington Avenue and Fifty-fourth Street, I met the man who would change my life.

I did not expect to be greeted by a casually dressed, boyish-looking Raymond K. Mason. When I looked at his shoestring tie and needlepoint belt, shock of reddish hair, and disarming smile, I wasn't sure what demeanor to adopt. Businesslike, serious, friendly …?

"Ah uhnderstand you have some ineresting adeahs for *American Home*," he began in a heavy Southern drawl. "Let's heah 'em."

I poured out my theory about the emerging American woman and the need for a new magazine to respond to her needs. He listened attentively, and my enthusiasm grew. "There are millions of housewives in America today who are being sold the same old tired homemaking advice, which only intensifies their dilemma. Even the new feminists preaching liberation love their families and want to do right by them. They need a magazine that delivers a philosophy that alleviates the pressure of outdated homemaking standards, one that speaks to them directly."

I was pitching for the job of editor; at no time did the financial aspects of the magazine come up.

Nor did Mason make any mention of the risks involved in changing a magazine's identity: loss of loyal readers who liked it as it was and loss of advertisers who resent the short-term loss of those readers.

Only later did I discover that Mason and the Charter Company had acquired American Home Publishing by assuming the liabilities, not an uncommon way of picking up a bargain. *American Home* was deeply in debt to Downe Communications and a subsidiary mail-order company. It was a tangled web of bad practices that had nothing to do with editorial credibility.

But I didn't know that then. I've often wondered if my naïveté wasn't an asset, if maybe I was hired over veteran publishers who would have been more familiar with the games.

As the interview ended, Mason called Ed Miller, president of Charter Publishing, to his office and said proudly, "Ed, Ah've found her. Heah is the next publisher of *American Home*."

Publisher I thought. *What is this man thinking?*

Miller somberly embraced me. "Congratulations, my dear, welcome aboard."

With no further executive protocol, Mason extended his hand, smiled and walked me to the door. "Mah secretary, Mary, will contact you."

My mind was spinning.

I knew about publishers—I had worked for one and was sleeping with one. Mort had just left his wife, and we were living together at the Phoenix. The publisher was a business manager, usually completely separate from the editorial side of the magazine. I knew little about ad sales and even less about magazine sales.

I hesitated, considering my options. I'd already interviewed at Condé Nast for an editorial position, and the human resources director had asked me to come in for a second interview.

I could probably land a job there as assistant to an editor at one of their established women's magazines. This was a crossroads. I could pursue Condé Nast and go the safe and traditional route, inching up the editorial ladder, dooming myself to middle-class servitude. Or I could expose myself to risk and maybe leap over a few rungs on that ladder of success.

Money was not the biggest issue. Breakthrough was—breakthrough into other strata of the magazine business.

Back home I listened to a phone message from Mason's office saying that a car would pick me up in the morning and take me to Butler Airfield in New Jersey. I would then fly to Mason's home in Jacksonville, Florida, where I would conclude negotiations for the job.

"Pack an overnight bag," the secretary said.

This was my first trip in a private jet. But it would not be the last.

As soon as I entered the spacious jet, partitioned neatly into sections, the door slammed behind me and the airline steward politely asked me to fasten my seat belt. I was dazzled by the swiftness and ease of boarding a private jet and by the instant takeoff.

Epping Forest, Mason's palatial home in Jacksonville, had formerly been the Alfred I. duPont estate. Nestled on the banks of Florida's St. John's River, this Spanish Renaissance mansion dated back to the twenties, as did other opulent European replicas built in Florida in the twenties and then abandoned with each economic downturn. Terraces and gardens bordered with cupids and other baroque statuary surrounded the fifteen thousand-square-foot residence, which sat on a fifty-eight-acre estate.

The house, which would never be free of the moldy odor it had acquired from being boarded up and uninhabited for decades, had clout nonetheless. Mason, as I would find out, effectively used his thirty-room residence to entertain the powerful and intimidate the aspiring.

The chauffeur drove smoothly up the winding driveway to the entry, where I was greeted by an English butler who led me to my room, with its giant four-poster bed requiring a step stool to enter.

As I unpacked, I felt like a princess fraud. Should I confess my inadequacies or just resolve to overcome them? The opportunity to take a moribund magazine with an existing base of 2.5 million, mostly women readers, and turn it around was irresistible. I believed in my editorial philosophy but viewed the business side of this venture with almost paralyzing fear.

When I descended the spiral stairway and entered the grand entryway, I was met by blonde and bubbly Minerva Mason, who greeted me in effusive Southern style. She gave me a tour of her home, and as we went from room to room, she meticulously explained the many mementoes and gifts from sheiks, princes, and the shah of Iran, all displayed in glass cases. Every available surface was crowded with silver-framed pictures of the Masons and their three children: on yachts, on balconies, on beaches, and always in the company of the high and mighty—Anwar Sadat, the shah of Iran, President Nixon. As the tour ended, we met Raymond Mason in the library.

If the trip to Epping Forest had been designed to dazzle me, it had succeeded. I soon learned that Mason was a fearless entrepreneur who had amassed a fortune in the oil business. He was recognized as a maverick businessman, reportedly with ties to the Saudi royal family. His mentor had been Ed Ball, trustee for the Alfred I. duPont estate.

Mason took me aside to explain his business philosophy, how he looked for certain characteristics in the people he hired. "Ah try to surround maself with people who 'git it' quickly and then act without waiting for puhmission. Can you do that? Do you believe in yourself enough tah take risks?"

I tried to clarify what a publisher does and why I believed my prior experience had not prepared me for that role. "The publisher is the business manager. She directs the sales staff, the magazine sales strategy, and has ultimate financial responsibility—"

Mason interrupted. "In mah view, the publisher is the star salesperson for the magazine. Now, who else can sell this ahdea behttar than you, since you ah the inventor? Just like you sold me, you'll have to teach all tha otha folks."

I nodded weakly. How brazen could I be?

"Now, ah want you to spend some time with my financial people. Among other things, they'll explain to you tha difference between P and L— profit and loss—and cash flow. You'll only worry about cash flow. Ma boys will take care of tha P and L."

So on a Tuesday in March in a bizarre villa in Florida, with a northeasterly wind whipping the trees and stirring the normally placid willows, I became the first woman publisher of a major American magazine with a circulation of more than one million. No contract, no promises, no country club membership. Just two people shaking hands. My salary was not discussed that day. An offer of $80,000 was made later in New York by Mason's financial vice president. I accepted. It was nearly double my previous salary.

Inexplicably, Raymond Mason and I trusted each other, and no matter what developed later, I would never forget the electrifying feeling of that day. I was in charge! A powerful, successful man who operated almost entirely on instinct believed that I had the ability and audacity to take on a job full of risk.

In the next two weeks, I finished up my work at *Men's Wear* and made the giant leap to the world of consumer magazines. Mort was both happy and jealous. I had preempted him, and his fragile ego was bruised. My departure relieved him of the sticky office situation but not his wife's ire. She sued him for divorce and intended to name me as correspondent. Only the intervention of a sharp New York lawyer prevented this and the headlines that would have besmirched my career before it had even started.

Now I was sitting in a corner office surrounded by plush furnishings and the latest office equipment.

I had inherited a complex dictating machine that was wired to my two secretaries' desks. This device filled me with awe, and to this day I miss it. After a brief tutorial from Marge, one of my secretaries, I was left alone to master it. I picked up the receiver and pushed the playback button, trying to test the unfamiliar object. Suddenly I heard John Mack Carter's voice on tape: "The root of the word *hysterical* is *hysterectomy*, which suggests the female nature of the condition. Men, by definition, cannot be hysterical."

What was that about? And is it true? I wondered. *Are women merely victims of their chemistry? Was Carter indicting women for an inability to control their emotions and behavior? And when did he dictate that?*

2. No More Cuckoo Clocks

I was soon yanked from my daydreams in my new corner office. Ed Miller, now the chairman of Charter Publishing (the Charter Company's subsidiary and American Home's parent) had scheduled a meeting to introduce me to the staff.

Forty people filed into my office and arranged themselves in order of their egos. The insecure hung back while the more confident stood smiling in the first row. Ed introduced me with enthusiasm, adding how lucky Charter was to have found me and what exciting times lay ahead. A quick read of the group's expressions did not reassure me that everyone was on board.

Then it was my turn. I felt confident in my Armani pantsuit.

Without belittling the magazine these people had been producing, and with a mixture of fear and bravura, I talked about the dawning of a new age and of the evolution of women's roles, cautiously avoiding the word *revolution*. My now-quivering voice spoke of a new woman who in many cases was juggling two roles, work and home.

"I believe the American woman needs to be rescued from unrealistic standards that hold her captive to housekeeping and make no allowance for her self-actualization. A contemporary women's magazine should not promote high-maintenance interior decorating. *American Home* has an opportunity to lead and redefine homemaking."

I told them my strategy would be revealed in the weeks ahead. "I welcome memos and input from anyone on how best we can accomplish this. Now is the time to express your ideas."

The door was open, the choice theirs. They could either enter or leave what many probably saw as the *Titanic*. The comparison was not unfair, considering the turbulent history of *American Home* and its declining readership and advertising revenue.

As the staff was filing out, Carlo Vittorini, newly appointed president of Charter Publishing, strode in. Wearing a dark Ivy League suit, white shirt, and narrow-striped rep tie, he was a striking figure. His crew cut and tawny skin revealed his American Indian roots rather than his Italian side, which he was clearly trying to minimize in order, I presumed, to comply with the publishing industry's WASP model for a publisher.

"Good morning, Leda. Ready to take charge?" he asked authoritatively, raising his outstretched open hand with a flourish that almost seemed like a slap.

"I'm looking forward to it, Carlo," I replied, smiling. "And I'm eager to hear what your priorities are." *Throw the ball back in his court,* I thought. Then another thought: *what a handsome man.*

"Well, the first item on your agenda should be understanding the serious circulation problem you've inherited. The circulation of *American Home* was over three million at its peak, but it's been declining rapidly. I suggest you meet with Chip Block, your circulation director, and have him bring you up to speed. He has some pretty definite ideas on what the strategy should be.

"Then you better have a sales meeting and get the best feedback you can from the salespeople. Also, call your regional reps and introduce yourself. They must be anxious about their positions.

"Finally, I understand you have some idea about changing the magazine's concept. I've heard a rumor that you're planning to target the magazine toward the so-called *new* woman. I would suggest you forget that for now. There's nothing wrong with the product. This magazine is almost a hundred years old. I would caution you to be careful about identifying the magazine with any radical ideas about women and society. We're not in the business of revolution. Leave that to the women's libbers. Now, do you have any questions?"

"Not at the moment, but I'm sure I will, and I'll call you. Thanks for your advice. I really look forward to working with you, Carlo. I've heard so much about you."

"Terrific, Leda. Here's my card. Call any time."

I wasn't surprised by Carlo's abrupt manner. Having earned the nickname "take-no-prisoners Vittorini," Carlo was an acknowledged chauvinist, accustomed to relegating women to the editorial arena and keeping firm control of finances.

It was the business side that worried me. I knew nothing about subscriber sales techniques or how to read circulation reports. And numbers were not my forte. I was a word person, a design person. Surely there would be specialists to oversee that part of the business.

Mason had assured me when I accepted the job that I would get all the support I needed and that Carlo would be there for me. He would be my mentor. Somehow I hadn't gotten that feeling from Carlo. In fact, I felt instinctively that he was not happy about my presence as publisher and that he might be my nemesis rather than my guardian angel.

* * *

Trying to avoid dwelling on the negative, I decided it was time to take a walk through the office and get to know the layout and staff. So I headed down the corridor that started at my corner office and divided the fifth floor of the Charter building.

Immediately on the left and parallel to my executive suite was the office of Helene Brown, the editor, followed by offices for the managing editor, the executive editor, and a group of editorial assistants. On the right was the large twenty-by-twenty-foot art department, home of the art director and two assistants, with drawing tables and cork wallboards. As this was before the computer age, people were not tethered to keyboards and screens. Some could actually draw.

At the end of the corridor, just before the reception area, was the advertising director's office, with a wall full of golf trophies and sports memorabilia. A little beyond that were dreary cubicles for the five ad-space salesmen and their secretaries. Uncomfortable workstations were deemed suitable for people who were supposed to be out of the office more than in. Out making a minimum of five calls a day, enjoying long martini lunches at Manhattan's best restaurants; in only to dictate letters and call reports for the publisher and to file their expense receipts for the day.

This was the age of paper and electric typewriters. The only other technical assistance a salesperson was allowed was a hand-held tape recorder. I soon discovered that the secretaries were surrogate mothers to many of our salesmen. It was not uncommon to hear a secretary calling a salesman's wife to tell her what he'd had for lunch—so she wouldn't duplicate it for dinner.

On the other side of the reception area were the offices of the circulation manager and the promotions department, as well as those of the American Home special publications division, with its own editor, Rachel Neuman.

And finally, at the very end of it all, were the comptroller and the accounting department. The sound of IBM Selectric typewriters and ringing phones provided a rhythmic background, music to some.

Having made the rounds, I returned to my office to begin the process of meeting individually with the staff.

The introduction of the new *American Home* was set for January 1976, the bicentennial year. It was now June, and with the standard three-month lead time required to produce a monthly magazine, that meant the new version would have to be ready to go to press in November. In addition, the editorial outlines and issue plans had to be in place at least three months before that so we could assign articles, schedule photography shoots, and determine the "book size"—the number of pages in an issue.

Firing and replacing the key editorial people could not be postponed. After reassuring Helene Brown, the editor, that she would be given every chance to prove herself, I asked for an evaluation of the editorial staffers. She wanted to keep them all.

Then I informed her that Joe, the art director, would be replaced by my art director from *Men's Wear*. "I'll introduce her to the staff tomorrow," I said.

"Oh my God!" She closed her eyes in the manner of someone with a splitting headache. "He's not going to take it well."

When I laid out my repositioning concept for the magazine, she naturally defended what they had been doing. "Leda, there are so many readers out there who love the *American Home* that John Mack Carter created. The old-fashioned, comfortable look of early-American furniture gives them a sense of security, and many love to make the crafts we offer."

"I'm sure you're right, Helene, but there aren't enough of those people to support the magazine financially and attract advertisers. You understand, don't you?"

Helene's survival instinct kicked in and she resisted no more.

When Joe entered my office hugging a bunch of editorial boards under his left arm, I knew Helene had not forewarned him. Before I could find the right words, he walked cautiously toward a paneled area with a shelf reserved for presentations.

He smiled, spread the boards on the ledge, and said, "Thought you'd like to see the October cover and the main well." The cover featured a blue stenciled chest of drawers with a pine rocking chair beside it, both sitting on a rust-colored hooked rug. The cover lines read: *A hooked rug you can make, Colonial bread recipes, Autumn in Williamsburg,* and *All-American house plans.*

As Joe continued the presentation, I tried to feign some interest without interrupting him. Finally I said, "Joe, please sit down."

Firing anyone is a grisly task. Joe's pain and confusion were palpable as I told him that because we were changing the editorial direction of the magazine, I felt I needed someone with a new artistic vision. My comforting words about how these things always work out for the best did not ring true, even to me. Joe was perspiring visibly and speechless.

"You are well respected in the business, Joe, and I'm sure you will find another job quickly. Helene will give you an excellent letter of recommendation. Good luck."

Joe awkwardly walked over to the shelf and attempted to gather the editorial boards, but his nervous hands made them slide off the ledge and land in a pile on the floor.

The next day I brought in Bettan Prichard, my former art director. She and I had been plotting the new direction for *American Home* for weeks. Her Scandinavian background enabled her to connect instantly with my ideas about simplicity in modern lifestyles. It was imperative that the magazine's visuals instantly communicate the new direction—away from hooked rugs and maple hutches lined with cute dishes. No more cuckoo clocks or dust-collecting curio cabinets.

I realized that I had introduced an element of discomfort into everyone's world. Moreover, they may have wondered if I'd been promoted because I was Raymond Mason's mistress; and if so, how much information would I be sharing with Mason?

As strange as it may sound, for me this mystery about my relationship with Mason was a kind of protection. For the time being.

3. A New American Woman

With no new media kits and only editorial boards illustrating the cover and contents of the magazine, I left on a cross-country sales trip to meet potential advertisers and to explain the new positioning of the magazine to regional sales forces. I wanted to show them firsthand how to promote the new *American Home*. My ammunition was my passionate enthusiasm for the idea. The corporate promotions director, Milt Franks, had assured me that would be enough for now.

I felt strongly we would find an audience for this new magazine, but I had no tangible evidence, no research that supported my premise. I would be relying heavily on innovative visuals, a sharp departure from the static and familiar design that dominated women's magazines, and provocative cover lines that challenged the norm.

What I hadn't anticipated but should have known was that the people who controlled the ad budgets were mostly middle-aged men with nuclear families and traditional outlooks. The magazine would challenge their status quo in more ways than one. The sales reps for *American Home* were also men, programmed to sell based on cost-per-thousand-readers, and they relied heavily on the allegiance of their buddies who controlled the ad budgets.

It was a man's world. And magazine ad sales was a man's game. The good ol' boys' network and the rapport they shared was very exclusive and permeated their conversations and actions. The bond of drinking buddies and sports analogies had nothing to do with the validity of an idea or a magazine's credo. It was about camaraderie that transcended the ideological theories I was going to present.

My first stop was Detroit, a visit to Whirlpool in nearby Benton Harbor and Kellogg in Battle Creek. Both were great American brands with a stake in the purchasing power of the American housewife. I also planned to stop at the big three auto companies. *American Home,* like most women's magazines of the era, carried no automotive advertising, but not for lack of trying. It was traditional to make a pitch to General Motors, Ford, and Chrysler anyway. The ad agencies advising the three behemoths lived by the conventional wisdom that it was inefficient to advertise automobiles to women because women were not the ones making the car-purchasing decisions. Other upstart magazines were also trying to break down these prejudices, to overturn fixed ideas about who made such decisions. *Ms. Magazine* was in the forefront trying to change perceptions, never an easy task.

In Detroit, I was met by a limousine driver and driven through the dark and deserted center of downtown to the St. Regis, a venerable old hotel on West Grand Avenue that had been built when Detroit was at the apex of its industrial glory. No one had warned me, though perhaps I should have known, that the city had not yet recovered from the riots of the 1960s.

The streets were desolate—not a person in sight. *Odd,* I thought, *for a major city.* "Where is everyone?" I asked the driver.

"Nobody goes to downtown Detroit anymore," he said. After a pause, he asked, "Why are you staying at the St. Regis? The magazine people all stay at the Michigan Inn on the lake."

He delivered this chillingly, I thought, like a line from a horror movie that makes everyone in the audience know something is coming. No one in New York had forewarned me. It was my first inkling that help would not be freely given by the employees I had inherited. I was on my own. So when I had informed the Detroit office that I would like to stay at the St. Regis, which was recommended in a travel guide, no one had enlightened me.

The next morning my driver picked me up and took me to D'Arcy McManus, the ad agency for Whirlpool, on the outskirts of the city. This would be the first test of my ability to sell the new *American Home.*

Dick Monley, the media director, greeted me with the warmth and grace that he was known for and that I very much needed then. My heart was racing as I began my presentation, my hands were trembling, my mouth dry.

"Well, my dear," Dick said as he reviewed the mockup of the magazine's new look, "This certainly is different. Do you think this is better and will attract enough new readers to maintain your circulation level?" Then, without breaking rhythm, he asked me how appliances would fit into the new environment.

"Well, Dick, I believe that women are waiting for a new style and approach to the basic concept of decorating the home. As for appliances, we intend to dramatize them, glamorize them, stimulate interest in an object that is normally looked at as just a necessity.

"I think we can generate some excitement and interest into the appliance category as no one ever has before. Our February issue is going to deliver an innovative and startling graphic presentation of the new refrigerator models for 1976. It's going to stop readers in their tracks."

As I spoke about the new contents and positioning of the magazine, I noticed sly delight on Dick's face. Perhaps it was relief after listening to years of redundant presentations. This was new, and it was fresh and bold. By the end of our meeting, I knew I had an ally.

It had been more than a decade since *American Home* had carried any Whirlpool ads, because it was what the industry considered the extra magazine in the crowded category of home improvement. *House Beautiful*, *House and Garden*, and *Better Homes & Gardens* were the leaders in the field.

"Now all you have to do is convince Dave Allen at Whirlpool," he said ominously.

I knew I needed help—and I got it later that day. I was joined by Chick Talley, the Midwest sales rep for the Charter group of magazines— *Ladies' Home Journal*, *Redbook*, *Sport*, and *Family Weekly*. It was my first opportunity to hear a veteran salesman make a presentation, and I was looking forward to it. I had so much to learn about the art of selling, and so much depended on my learning it quickly.

Waiting in the reception room at Whirlpool, Chick and I were surrounded by other salespeople, all men, all with large presentation cases. Most of the men knew each other and babbled away boisterously about this golf tournament or that football game. This was my introduction to the sports jargon that unfailingly punctuated the conversations of these good ol' boys. It was the kind of talk that encouraged a sense of being part of an inner circle. And I was on the outside in every way because I did not like sports and couldn't even feign interest. I wondered if I would ever be accepted as a member of this exclusive club.

Finally it was our turn. We entered the conference room to face the decision makers, Dave Allen and his media department. After we made our presentation, the questions began with targeted intensity.

"How are you going to transition an audience of two million to this new product?"

"You're bound to lose readers who will refuse to accept the new magazine. How will you make that up? Will you still meet our guaranteed circulation base?"

"What research systems do you intend to use to gauge our success or failure?"

Chuck jumped in aggressively, exuding enthusiasm for the new magazine and the team guiding it. I too joined in and brought the conversation back to the new design and the more dramatic aspects of the publication. I showed them our ads, to be launched in January 1976, which declared, "Happy Birthday, America. We have a new magazine for you!"

My diversion worked. Staring goggle-eyed at the rather risqué cover photo of a man and a woman lying on a bed, each with a glass of wine in hand, they forgot their questions and their doubts—for now. A month later we found out that Whirlpool had agreed to advertise with us in 1976—the first time in ten years.

* * *

Accompanied by Pat Dougherty, our other Midwest sales rep, I traveled on to Chicago, where the meetings moved in a polished, orderly way. Pat's manners were almost courtly, but his conservative mindset did not prevent him from enthusiastically introducing me and my "radical" ideas about the new woman. He was a seasoned salesman who had survived the management turnover at *American Home*. He sympathized with my situation. Consequently, he would prep me extensively before each meeting, and I believe he encouraged his clients to welcome me warmly.

As we made the rounds of the ad agencies, I came to feel more at home in Chicago. It was the beginning of a love affair. Over the years, my affection for the city would only grow. I love its mix of old and new architecture, its dramatic location on the edge of a lake that stretches to the horizon like a vast sea.

My next stop was Los Angeles. Suzanne Douglas, the L.A. rep, and I hit it off immediately. She understood that promoting the new *American Home* was natural for a woman to be able to do well. She instinctively understood the audience we would be targeting because she was one of them. An emancipated female who had been one of the first women to break into magazine ad sales, she was a tall, ebullient blonde with a hearty laugh.

Her ability to embrace the new message vividly underscored the need for me to make changes in the sales force. Although the New York salesmen I had inherited were adept at quoting rate-card statistics, they lacked the emotional fire required to convince advertisers to take a chance on a new idea. My goal now was to locate more women qualified to sell. Suzanne and I laughed a lot as we traversed the L.A. network of highways while sharing our ideas on the emerging new woman, modern men, single life, and much more.

In the Los Angeles area, most of our advertising prospects were in the food business. Their main concern was what percentage of editorial space would be devoted to recipes, particularly recipes that included the ingredients they were promoting. I learned to my surprise that dozens of boards—the Raisin Board, the Almond Board, the Peach Board—allocated their limited advertising dollars to magazines that utilized their product as ingredients in their recipes. Each year they sent magazines a questionnaire to help them calculate how many recipes featured the nut or fruit they promoted. That's how they stimulated sales for the item the growers paid them to promote. Thus, raisins appeared in the most unlikely recipes, and to this day those recipes are passed on to new generations of cooks, who can only wonder why raisins often appear in the mashed sweet potatoes.

With Suzanne I drove countless miles, crisscrossing the sprawling Los Angeles megalopolis from this agency to that company headquarters. I was introduced to California's whimsical cuisine and to cilantro, an herb I have never learned to like. From Suzanne I also learned who was sleeping with whom and who to be on guard against.

Bob Weber, our other West Coast rep, met me in San Francisco, where we maintained an office along with our sister publications. Bob had arranged the usual trip through the wine country, although there was virtually no wine advertising in magazines in those days.

Winery ad budgets were small, as was the industry. The boutique wineries in Napa and Sonoma could barely afford a few inches of space in the back of *Gourmet* magazine. Only Gallo in Modesto and Almaden south of San Francisco had advertising budgets of any meaningful size. So this trip was considered a perk for tired publishers.

After a night at the Stanford Court in San Francisco, we drove north over the Golden Gate Bridge. This is when I caught my first glimpse of the little town of Sausalito nestled at the foot of the Marin headlands. The green hills, the sparkling blue water, the curve of the Bay struck me with full force.

"It looks like Italy," I blurted to Bob.

"Really? I've never been there."

Bob had arranged a luncheon for us with Robert Mondavi at the Mondavi Winery in Napa. We would then have dinner with Sam Sebastiani of Sebastiani Winery and his wife at their country home.

Robert Mondavi and Margrit, then his public relations manager, rolled out the red carpet for us. They already had a clear vision of how to promote California wines, and Margrit fully grasped the value of public relations. Many of the people we met at the wineries were of Italian ancestry, and they warmed to me when they found out I was Italian and could speak the language.

Sitting outside on the patio of the sun-splashed Mondavi Winery, I let the warm soft air of the wine country wash over me. *What a contrast to Detroit, Chicago, and Los Angeles,* I thought. The endless rows of well-manicured vines reminded me of Tuscany, reviving memories of my year there as a fifteen-year-old, especially of walks in the Italian countryside and meals al fresco under a grape arbor.

As we drove back to San Francisco, I resolved to return to northern California some day—not just on business, but to live. It was the closest place I could find to Tuscany without having to move back to Italy.

Flying back to New York in the first-class cabin of the TWA 747 made me feel pampered. I was enjoying this respite from the office. Traveling as publisher of a major magazine in those days was better than a luxury vacation. You were given the royal treatment, you met interesting people, and you saw the world on the company expense account. I could get used to this, I decided.

Of course, it wasn't all fun. Even on the plane there was work to do. I opened my briefcase, found my writing pad, and began to write a summary of sales activity. Then I composed rough versions of follow-up letters to the advertisers and ad agency people I'd met with. I wrote everything in longhand on a lined yellow pad, a habit I still maintain today.

My first letter went to Bill Harmon at J. Walter Thompson, the Chicago ad agency representing Philip Morris. Wooing a tobacco company made me feel like a hypocrite. I had always hated cigarettes and felt in fact they should be outlawed rather than promoted. But this was the age of the Marlboro man, and one of the most visible signs of women's emancipation was the ad campaign for Virginia Slims. Their tag line, "You've come a long way, baby," was clearly aimed at the new woman.

My thoughts were reinforced by the smoke drifting under my nose from the nearby smoking section. *On the other hand*, I thought, *my personal feelings aren't really relevant here.* We were courting Philip Morris because they were a major advertiser. Tobacco advertising dollars were a mainstay for other magazines, and we needed the ad revenue until other product advertisers were found. But where would the new business come from? Appliances? Home-improvement products? Sadly, no one in the home improvement field had advertising budgets comparable to those of tobacco companies.

I reclined my seat, stretched out, and closed my eyes. It had been an exciting first few months and a stimulating week of travel. My thoughts drifted away from my new life and back to my old one. The one I'd left in North Pelham, New York.

* * *

Six years before, I'd led my two children down the front steps of my beautiful colonial home with the brass eagle on the front door.

"Where are we going to live, Mommy?" Robert asked.

"I told you, Robby. We're going to live at grandma's house."

"But I don't want to live at grandma's house. I like our house."

My eyes filled with tears as I relived that day. How could I do this to my family? Break a promise to a good husband? Disrupt my children's lives? But then I heard another voice: How can I not? Simply put, I had reached the limit of my endurance, an abiding intolerance for the very life I had once craved.

When did it all change? What made me turn against the "good life" in the idyllic suburbs and demand more?

It hadn't happened suddenly but rather over years. In the early days of my marriage to Howard, I'd felt a dissatisfaction, an ennui, the likes of which I'd only read about in books.

It had happened long before 1963, when Betty Freidan sounded a call to revolution for women like me, cosseted housewives caring for husbands and children, women with no separate identity or income. Emerson, Thoreau, and Camus had inflamed my passion for a life beyond service to the family. What I heard was an existential call to arms, no matter the price. It was as if their very words were calling directly to me. "The unexamined life is not worth living," Socrates had declared two thousand years ago, and I now believed this wholeheartedly.

Nestled in the embrace of my soft airplane seat, I dug deeper to find out what had driven me to change my life.

I certainly had grown bored with the dull repetitiveness of daily life. The predictability, the sense of powerlessness, the constant disciplining of children—it finally got to me. I had tried, made efforts to expand my life. I attended watercolor classes and poetry classes. I even taught Sunday school at the Huguenot Presbyterian Church in Pelham, now that I had rejected Catholicism and become a Presbyterian. Still, excitement and challenge eluded me, as did stimulating conversation.

Howard was a quiet and sweet man, and when I finally told him that I couldn't take the quiet anymore, he confessed that he had married me in the hope that I would help him become more interesting and talkative. Clearly, being married to me had had the opposite effect. As I entered my thirties, I became ever more caustic and critical. I didn't like the way he chewed his food, and not unlike the scene in the movie

War of the Roses, that small detail of life put me on edge in a totally irrational way.

Life was too predictable with Howard, conversationally and sexually. Was there in fact a subterranean sexual fever behind my restlessness? Or had I simply outgrown my husband? Whatever the reason, I had lost the will to make sacrifices anymore. I no longer possessed the basic Christian ability to put my family's needs before my own.

With the children in the backseat and Felix the cat cowering in his carrier, we drove the short distance to my family's Tudor mansion on Cliff Avenue, also in Pelham, but on the more affluent side of town. It was not a bad place to transition from one life to another.

Living with my family—grandmother, grandfather, mother, aunt, uncle, and cousin—gave me a sense of security. My children would be safe while I looked for work. Ensconced in the twenty-room house— complete with live-in maid, spiral staircase, and billiard room—my kids would not suffer from lack of resources or attention. And my Tuscan grandmother would happily prepare delicious Italian meals for us.

Finding a job was the real challenge. I had been out of the workforce for years. I knew I didn't want to go back to the fashion industry. After graduating from the Fashion Institute of Technology, I had worked in a couple of dismal jobs as designer's assistant at the low end of the garment business. What I really wanted was a chance to get into the magazine publishing business. But how could I do that without a journalism degree? My only hope was to get an entry-level position and learn on the job.

One of my last jobs before I had children had been in a studio that provided design services for the children's wear industry. I made an appointment with Harold Engleman, the owner of the studio. Sad to hear about the breakup of my marriage, he listened attentively to my story and then immediately called Ted Tarlow, publisher of *Teens & Boys Outfitter,* the magazine of the boys' wear industry.

Ted was an exuberant, imposing man. Vowing not to be intimidated, I showed him all I had: a scrapbook of articles I'd written for the local Pelham paper and my sincere and unrestrained enthusiasm. He responded, hiring me as assistant to the editor, Lew Spalding. This was my first lesson in the importance of communicating passionate interest in a job. The job was to cover the boy's wear market by calling on the manufacturers, looking at their lines, and reporting on the trends. I vowed I would work tirelessly to prove myself. And I did. *Teens & Boys* was where I learned about magazine production.

Six years later, I was flying first class.

4. THE HAPPY HOUSECLEANER

Back in New York, I was overwhelmed with the complex requirements of learning how to run a multimillion-dollar publishing business. I read every business periodical I could, as well as the newsletters that fed the gossip mill about the industry.

I found my name often and usually in a derogatory way. Dubbed "the happy housecleaner" because of my reorganization of the company, I was an easy target for antifeminist rhetoric. The high-priced industry newsletters, such as *Media Industry Newsletter* (*MIN*) and the *Gallagher Report*, thrived on innuendoes and insider scoops that did not require substantiation. Rumors about discontent in the ranks due to my "dictatorial" management style were relished by the competition.

Mort would minimize the importance of the criticism and buoy my spirits with his raunchy Jewish humor. While these jokes are not worth repeating, they always elicited the laughter I needed.

Despite the excitement I derived from my role at *American Home*, I was torn. My sons, both teenagers, caused me concern. Scott, fourteen, didn't like the exclusive boys' school I'd managed to get him into despite his lack of pedigree. Although Browning School (at Sixty-first and Park Avenue) was highly touted, it was located in a Gothic stone building, its classrooms devoid of sunlight.

After school, Scott had nowhere to ride his bicycle on Sixty-fifth Street, and no way would I let him ride in Central Park alone. He longed for the suburbs, and I felt guilty for having sacrificed his quality of life for mine.

Robert, nineteen, had dropped out of the New Haven School of Criminology, disillusioned by the behavior of many of the students who were studying to become police officers. Their commitment to law and order did not extend to their personal behavior, which was characterized by drinking and rowdiness. It was a pure animal house.

In retrospect I realize that Robert was not ready to go away to college. He missed home and one day just showed up with all his belongings strapped to the roof of his car and announced he was never going back. Although he gave up on his dream of becoming a cop, he never ceased to be enamored with the police and their work. To this day he has police radios in his car and regularly listens to their communications.

In an effort to get Robert interested in something else, I hired him as a production assistant at *American Home*. He worked with a kindly magazine veteran, Ferdinand d'Esposito, who took pleasure in mentoring him.

In my enthusiasm to make changes and see quick results, I made mistakes at *American Home*. They contributed to my growth and learning, though that was hard to see at the time. The alternative would have been to pretend, to conceal my inexperience. I have found over my lifetime that people in business waste a lot of time and energy pretending to be more accomplished than they are, thereby not asking the right questions or preparing for the possibility of being found out. Raymond Mason had encouraged me to trust my instincts and "never explain and never complain." It was good advice that served me well.

Another important lesson I learned from Mason was the value of having one excellent executive secretary rather than the two adequate ones I had inherited.

"Ledah," he'd said, "there's nothing that can replace one really great secretary. You have no ahdea how this can increase y'all's efficiency. Ahm going to send you someone I know you will like. Her name's Shirley Bailey. She was Robert Vesco's executive secretary. His right arm. You know, Nixon's pal? The stock scammer who fled to Costa Rica in 1973. But she can't find work right now because he's under investigation and no one wants to get embroiled in that mess. His name is not a good reference."

As Mason promised, Shirley became the dream secretary who anticipated my every need and increased my efficiency. She also became my ear to the office scuttlebutt. There was no shortage of rumors circulating. One of the hottest was that the editor of *Sport* magazine, Dick Schapp, was having an affair with one of our pretty salespeople, Trish McCloud. That one turned out to be true.

Shirley also developed a maternal relationship with my sons, providing me with assurance that we were always connected even when I was on the road. She was the conduit, the link, the monitor, who gave me the peace of mind I needed to focus on work.

In January of 1976, the revamped, repositioned, new-and-improved *American Home* appeared on the newsstands and in mailboxes around the country. Full-page ads in the *New York Times*, *Adweek*, *Ad Age*, the *Chicago Tribune*, and the *Los Angeles Herald* announced the new magazine. In it we had capitalized on the bicentennial mood of the country.

"Happy Birthday, America. We have a new magazine for you!" our ads shouted. They featured a blowup of the January cover with its seductive image: a beautiful brunette holding a glass of wine while lying on a bed beside an attractive man. The single cover line was a departure from the formulaic multiple cover lines dictated by magazine distributors and supposedly required to sell magazines on newsstands. It stated boldly, "Everything you can do in the bedroom," implying more than readers found in the actual article, which simply acknowledged that people were eating in bed, watching TV in the bedroom, and no longer abiding by the old rules. It had been developed by Milt Franks, the promotion director of Charter Publications. Deliberately provocative, it was calculated to stimulate newsstand sales.

It was an iconoclastic approach for a home-service magazine, and it startled some subscribers and advertisers, who were unprepared for such a dramatic change of appearance in this American classic. A big leap from butter churns, spinning wheels, and cozy cover lines about life in Williamsburg to a sensuous cover photo complete with double entendre. But the message was clear and the course was set. This was a new magazine for a new woman who needed and deserved a better recipe for facing the challenge of living a dual life with new priorities.

I remember 1976 not only as a celebration of our nation's birth, but also as the year when I elevated my understanding of the publishing business. For the first time, I saw the enormous chasm that separates the worker bees and the financial decision makers, perhaps in any business. Magazine publishing is first and foremost a business, with financial objectives that are disconnected from the creative aspects, the area that attracts—or should attract—imaginative young people to work for magazines. As I write this, the future of print hangs in the balance, and this saddens me.

Sitting in endless, mind-numbing meetings on advertising, circulation, and production costs tested my powers of concentration. My mind often wandered as the men droned on …

I wondered if I would have gotten this far if my name were my maiden name, Giovannetti, instead of Sanford. Leda Maria Giovannetti—it had a nice ring, but it probably would have disqualified me for an executive position in the publishing world in the seventies. It screamed Italian, conjuring some negative stereotypes. But I was under the radar then. *Sanford* projected Waspish legitimacy, the right name to go at the top of the masthead. I was camouflaged by my ex-husband's name.

As I slowly got up to speed on the tricky equation that was necessary to extract profit from a failing business, I realized there was another bottom line that I did not have access to. The original direction from Mason about concentrating on cash flow and not profit and loss became clear. All I had to worry about was the operating expenses and how to generate income from advertising and magazine sales. The accountants would focus on calculating P and L in their own creative way.

Over the years, I found that characteristic of all the financial executives and number crunchers I worked with—a chicanery masked by sly charm designed to make you feel comfortable. People who worship at the accounting shrine seldom have soul or imagination.

In contrast to the deadly business planning sessions, our editorial planning meetings were exciting and alive. We briskly exchanged fresh new ideas and planned artistic approaches to bring to life a fresh new vision of the American home.

On the sales side, I replaced each male salesman with a woman, except for one elderly man whom I feared might not find another job. He rewarded me with total commitment to the new *American Home*.

Behind the scenes, the editor and some of the employees at our sister publication, *Ladies' Home Journal*, were funneling negative information to Mason about morale at *American Home*. To his credit, Mason always shared the feedback and asked me what was really going on.

Then, while in Los Angeles on a sales trip, I received a call from Mason saying that he wanted to pick me up and fly me to Paris with him. This would give us some time to review the status and temperature of *American Home*. Did I have my passport with me? No. Could I have Shirley get it to him and he would bring it? I was staying in Mason's private cottage at the exclusive Bel Air Hotel in Beverly Hills.

I called Mort, told him about the invitation, and asked him to get my passport from the top dresser drawer and messenger it to Shirley. Mort was not happy about this. He never really enjoyed my success, and now he was jealous of this high-level invitation. As he saw it, his protégé had passed him by and was about to experience something he'd never known.

"Just you and him?" Mort's voice had an edge to it. "How cozy."

When I said nothing, he added sarcastically, "Guess you have a lot of business to discuss on such a long flight. Well, just be sure to bring me back some Cuban cigars. And hide them well, because you go through customs even on a private plane."

A limo driver picked me up and drove me to a small airfield, where Mason's Grumman 2 was waiting. As I walked up the stairs and into the womb of the expansive jet, much larger than the one that had transported me to Florida, my body tingled with excitement. Mason greeted me warmly with a handshake, and then we took off. The thrill of entering a world of luxury and privilege cannot be overstated.

Sitting in plush swivel armchairs, we drank Cokes. Mason never touched alcohol, and I rarely drank in those days except for an occasional whiskey sour before dinner in a restaurant.

With his disarming Southern drawl, Mason began to review the activities at *American Home*. He spoke of the necessary staff changes, the controversial editorials, and the fact that newsstand sales were increasing, but not fast enough.

"Ledah, can you explain these figures to me? Why do we have to spend $1.2 million to send mail to six million folks to get back 300,000 or so subscriptions? It seems mighty expensive to me. And we're even offering a first prize of a furnished house, plus all those other prizes. Won't they buy a $5.95 subscription without a sweepstake?"

"Well, Raymond," I said (Mason insisted I call him Raymond), "I've asked that of Chip and Al. They told me we must replace the 300,000 subscribers who don't renew or we have to lower our rate base. As you know, that's the number of people we guarantee will receive and read the magazine. That would mean we have to lower the price of a page of advertising. Result: we suffer lost revenue from the subscribers and reduced revenue from the ad side."

I surprised myself with my ability to recite what had been Greek to me just a few months ago.

"But we'll print fewer copies, won't we? So we'll reduce expenses," Raymond countered.

"Yes, that's true, but then we have to deal with our credibility on Madison Avenue. And right now they're watching us like hawks. Any sign of weakness and we'll further jeopardize our ability to build ad sales. Then we'd have to give rebates to advertisers for not meeting our circulation guarantee. A cut in circulation would be a sign of weakness."

After a pause, he simply mumbled, "A-uh."

We continued to discuss the various aspects of the business until Mason, with characteristic boyish enthusiasm, proclaimed, "It's the cost of printing, right? That's the biggest cost. That's what we have to control!"

With that he seemed to connect the dots to the business opportunity he had been presented. He went on: "Carlo has informed me that Dayton Press, the largest printing plant in the country, is for sale. Ah understand that David Mahoney, the owner, is looking to sell. Perhaps we should buy it."

As the steward set the table for dinner, Mason kept returning to options for cutting costs and upping revenue. "Ledah, why don't you visit Dayton, and then we'll make an offer. They can be our bank."

Speechless, I just nodded.

After we stopped to refuel in Gander, Newfoundland, the steward lowered and made our beds. There was a seductive and glamorous quality to this experience that would leave me with an appetite for more.

In the morning, we arrived in Paris and were driven to the George V Hotel, considered by many the most deluxe hotel in Paris. I had never been in such a sumptuous hotel setting.

On my own that day, I wandered the enchanting streets of Paris, finally locating a newsstand that sold Cuban cigars. After buying a box for Mort, I sat at a sidewalk café near the Louvre and ate a *petit* ham and cheese baguette and drank an espresso. I have been searching for one as delicious ever since.

That evening we dined in the Tuileries Gardens. Mason ordered the same entrée he always ordered—steak. The evening was magical, the conversation stimulating. Although Mason exuded a unique kind of magnetism that was based on power, he held no attraction for me, even with the support of such a romantic setting. If he was disappointed that this date did not evolve into a seduction, he did not express it.

My trip to Paris, no secret in the New York offices of Charter Communications, fueled the jealously and suspicion that was already in the air.

Mort accepted his cigars as small compensation for what he was certain had been a tryst.

5. The Corporate Jungle

I should have realized when I was asked to go to Ohio to look over the facilities of Dayton Press I was part of an elaborate charade. How could I possibly evaluate a printing facility? Why me? For the staff at *American Home*, it reinforced my position of authority. For me personally, it was a waste of time.

But that was what Mason "recommended" I do when we returned from Paris, and so I did. I was fully committed to learning on the job while following orders. I was mastering the art of posturing with confidence, a quality that seems to come so naturally to successful businessmen.

My trip was a formality that would make it appear as if some thought and investigation had gone into the plan to acquire Dayton Press. In reality it was a fait accompli.

David Mahoney, chairman of Norton Simon, had charmed Mason into believing that controlling the printing side of the business was one avenue to success in the magazine world. Carlo had also pushed the deal. Norton Simon was a conglomerate that owned Dayton Press. Mason had been told that great efficiencies would now accrue to Charter Publications and especially to *American Home*. Like so many deals, this one had been conceived at a cocktail party in the Windows on the World at the top of one of the Twin Towers in lower Manhattan.

In that same social setting, Mahoney and Carlo had convinced Mason that besides acquiring Dayton Press, he should buy *Redbook*, which was also owned by Norton Simon. It was a package deal. The key to this transaction was that the printer would become "the bank," providing credit for Charter. But in fact, behind the scenes there was a strategy I was not privy to till the magazine folded. The idea was to consolidate the two magazines into one publication. The two million readers of *American Home* would be added to *Redbook*'s circulation, reducing mailing costs and making it a more efficient advertising buy. *Redbook* would acquire two million readers and raise its rate base at no cost. The *American Home* name would be incorporated into the *Redbook* label. Subscribers to *American Home* would be offered *Redbook* as an alternative or their money back, a common practice in magazine publishing.

Meanwhile, I turned to Ferd d'Esposito to help me prepare for my road trip. "Dayton is the most antiquated printing plant in the U.S.," d'Esposito said. "It's being crippled by a labor dispute. The unions constantly block automation and impede every attempt at modernization. It's a white elephant. We have contracts with them for all the Charter magazines, and those contracts are pretty solid."

Great, I thought. *What can I do?*

Armed with this minimal information, I flew to Dayton. I was met by the manager of the mammoth facility and then the president. As I walked through the plant, which was a mile long, I tried to look interested and knowledgeable. It was a noisy beehive of activity, with the presses grinding away and trains clacking in and out, bringing in paper and other materials required to produce magazines and taking out the finished ones.

The plant manager periodically spewed angry rhetoric about how the unions were preventing him from modernizing the plant and acquiring the technology that would make them more efficient and thus competitive with other printers. "Damn it, how the hell are we supposed to stay in this business? We can't compete because of labor costs, which could be reduced if we were allowed to automate. Sorry for the cuss words, Ms. Sanford. But you understand what I'm saying?"

"Yes, I do, and no need to apologize." I didn't know what else to say.

My first and last thought: *Why didn't we just negotiate a new contract with another printer?* As I learned later, getting out of this agreement, which involved all the Charter publications, was not only fraught with penalties but would increase manufacturing costs and force us to raise the cover price of the magazines (*American Home* cost seventy-five cents). Perhaps owning the printer was the solution.

Back in New York, I could only report that I had indeed been there. Sending the publisher made the visit seem like a serious attempt at evaluating the situation prior to management's next move.

In fact, it signaled the beginning of the end.

Mason soon brought another player on the scene: Jack Trescott, one of Mason's wily southern buddies. With no publishing background, Trescott immersed himself in the business and began to develop a plan to overcome our financial problems. In the hope of forging a stronger team, Mason decided to hold a retreat at his home in Ireland for top management.

The publishers and editors-in-chief were flown to Shannon on Mason's Grumman 2. It was a heady experience, standing in an airplane having cocktails as if we were in an earthbound lounge. Standing next to Lenore Hershey, editor-in-chief of *Ladies' Home Journal*, I tried to relate to her but found myself distracted by her face. The blue line around her colorless eyes was uneven and blurred; the rouge on her doughy cheeks had been clumsily blended, and worst of all, she was talking with her mouth full of puff pastry.

"You know, we have an exclusive with Barbara Walters on the January cover," she sputtered. "She looks fabulous."

Lenore had risen to her eminent position via the public-relations route. Her famous Rolodex, bulging with the phone numbers of the rich and famous, was her main contribution to the celebrity-addicted women's service magazine field.

She turned her glare on me with visible suspicion. "So, Leda, what little surprise do you have up your sleeve for the *American Home* readers?" she asked.

I deflected the question with thinly disguised sarcasm. "Lenore, nothing to top your scoops."

Once in Ireland, we were driven to Ballynahinch Castle in Galway for our three-day conference. I quickly began to feel uncomfortable, as we do when we sense we're not being embraced by others. The planning meetings, which I assumed would be an open discussion of my ideas, elicited mutterings, frowns, and furtive glances of displeasure or dismay.

Apparently *American Home* did not have any fans in the corporate family.

Meetings were held in the mornings, with afternoons set aside for play. After lunch, Carlo paired off with his cronies while I was left to hike in the beautiful countryside with some of the minor executives. The poetic green Irish hills and cliffs by the sea were punctuated by castle ruins and crumbling abbeys, verifying all those corny songs about Ireland.

If the retreat was calculated to forge a team spirit, it didn't work. We were split into two camps—the majority, committed to the status quo and self-preservation, and the minority, a few of us who really wanted to shake up the order of things to create a new and vital company. As usual, the idealists didn't have a chance.

"Why do you persist in promoting this image of a new American woman, Leda?" Carlo challenged me one morning. "Where is your research to support this?"

"Carlo, if we want to substantiate this, we need to invest in research. But I haven't been allocated a budget for that. In lieu of that, we can invent a marketing story. We can find plenty of statistics that confirm a shift in the lifestyles of the emerging woman—for example, more women working, lower birth rate, and higher sales of books targeting their demographic. Corporate Promotion Director Milt Franks can do this, just as he did when he invented the eighteen-to-thirty-four market."

Carlo was expressionless, as usual; I jumped in deeper.

"Carlo, you remember how *Redbook* was struggling to compete among women's service magazines? How it was considered superfluous for advertisers who wanted to reach young women? Then Milt developed this mythical demographic segment. By manipulating available statistics, *Redbook* could claim to reach the eighteen-to-thirty-four female magazine buyers most efficiently."

Carlo appeared to be listening, but he gave no clue what he was thinking.

"So," I continued, "we have to be willing to challenge the editorial premise of our sister magazine, *Ladies' Home Journal,* with its focus on celebrity."

Lenore's face flushed, and Lou Porterfield, the *Ladies' Home Journal* publisher, also reddened.

Later at lunch, I could see the *LHJ* executives huddled over their Irish stew, casting unfriendly glances my way. I thought of one of Mort's favorite sayings: "Tell them what they want to hear." I knew it was good advice, but I couldn't follow it. I believed in what I was saying, so I kept saying it. And the antagonism I elicited grew.

As I eventually discovered, it wouldn't have mattered whether my ideas were good or bad. The entrenched employees at *Ladies' Home Journal* and *Redbook* were threatened because I had disrupted the order of things and garnered the support of the king of the castle (literally). I had to be done away with.

At dinner, ample drinking helped people let their guard down. Those relaxed moments of revelry were punctuated with stories about Irish drinking habits. Most featured a beleaguered Irish woman literally carrying her husband out of one pub or another. Meanwhile, a similar scene played out in the lobby of Ballynahinch Castle each evening. The notoriously bad Irish food was no doubt one reason liquor was consumed so heavily before dinner. Another reason: no wine was served during the meal.

The seating at the round tables in the castle's adjoining small dining rooms allowed us to converse and share what we had seen and heard that day. Listening to the conversations, I sensed a camaraderie I did not share. I'd never be an insider, I realized. I didn't drink, I hadn't climbed the ladder the traditional way, and I didn't respect the accepted order of things. Three strikes.

"I thought we came all the way to Ireland to do some creative brainstorming," I said to Jack Trescott one day when no one else was around. We were leaning against one of the stone balconies of the castle. "I thought this was going to be a stimulating few days that would recharge us all."

"Sorry you're disappointed, Leda, but I don't think you really understand that this is about bonding—bonding with people who may totally disagree with you. And you're not doing a good job. It's a political game, and you want to play it straight."

Trescott was right. I was naïve if I thought I could convert them to my way of thinking about anything, let alone the improvement of magazine publishing. There were no new ideas to be exchanged here, only platitudes and small talk about golf and family life.

Another target of conservative animosity was *Women's Sports*, Billie Jean King's magazine, which was part of the Charter publishing family, barely. It too had been slow in gaining advertising support and building circulation and thus was losing favor with management. A few indelicate remarks about Billy Jean's sexual preferences slipped out in the relaxed evening hours. But little was said about the publication itself. That very neglect identified it as a lesser star in the Charter firmament.

Each night I lay in bed, wondering how I could present my brilliant ideas so as not to antagonize the old guard further. Should I smile more at the very people who looked at me with stone faces? Should I agree with those who espoused ideas I detested?

Eventually my thoughts turned to happier matters. *What's Mort doing tonight?* I wondered. I missed his touch, his quips, his comforting words. I recalled the early days of our affair, our illicit, late-night encounters at business conventions not unlike this one. Why should this retreat be any different? Mutual attraction, alcohol, spousal absence, romantic setting—surely some caved to the temptation. Unable to sleep, I listened for footsteps, imagining who might be moving to who's room. Once, those footsteps had been mine.

6. SCANDAL

Six months had passed since my installation as publisher and editor-in-chief of *American Home*, and I woke up each morning with a growing enthusiasm for my job—soon followed by the reoccurring fear that one false move could send me plummeting to the bottom of the ladder.

I liked the power and relished the responsibility, while always conscious that the corridors of the Downe building at 420 Lexington Avenue, which housed *Ladies' Home Journal, WomenSports, Sport, Family Weekly,* and American Home Publishing, were a web of intrigue. Before the advent of e-mail and Blackberries, instant messaging was done live via gossip in hallways and around water coolers.

From the outside I watched as my idols, Gloria Steinem and Pat Carbine, struggled to launch *Ms. Magazine*, and another upstart company started *Working Woman*. The original concept of women's service magazines was being challenged. (Sadly, forty years later, only a few magazines, such as Oprah's *O*, have broken the mold.)

In February 1977, I flew to Dallas, to the National Association of Homebuilders convention, excited about attending the largest homebuilding products show in the world. This would be my first opportunity to promote the new version of the magazine directly to the leaders in the field of home design and to prove my ability to sell the new *American Home* to manufacturers. My previous proselytizing had been confined to ad agencies.

American Home was exhibiting an innovative new concept developed in conjunction with the Kohler Company. We would focus on the romantic aspect of a new bathtub large enough for two, available with a Jacuzzi option. The headline for the article, "Two's Company," was in keeping with the Valentine's Day theme of the February issue.

For that same issue, I had interviewed Bob Guccione, the publisher of *Penthouse*, a move appreciated neither by many Charter executives nor by many of our middle-America readers. The interview, entitled "Sex in the Seventies," contributed to my budding reputation as a radical women's libber determined to tear down American family values. My questions and Guccione's answers were outrageous for the time, and rereading them today makes me wonder where I got the chutzpah to do that interview.

I asked Guccione about guilt: "If morality changes and if younger people are more natural and less hampered by a lot of the hang-ups that afflict our generation, will guilt then disappear?"

His reply: "As women become more liberated and acquire many of the interests that men have now, that men have enjoyed traditionally, society will have to meet the demands of the individual, and morality will have to change. Guilt is the result of the collision between the individual's attempt to express his or her individuality and the social order."

This may not sound too racy today, but in the context of a magazine called *American Home*, catering to an audience of middle-class American housewives in 1977, it rocked their world. Letters poured in from disturbed subscribers, mostly in the heartland of America, many canceling their subscriptions.

I could have taken the safe road and guided the magazine on a more moderate path, but something was prodding me to challenge the establishment in the only way I knew how, or had the power to do.

* * *

With copies of the January 1977 edition of *American Home* tucked in my Gucci briefcase, I wandered through the crowd from one exhibit to the other.

As I reached the dazzling Kohler exhibit filled with avant-garde toilets and bathtubs, their brass fixtures gleaming, I spotted an imposing and handsome man who was holding court, surrounded by an attentive crowd. I have always nurtured a romantic image of the male idol, one that harks back to those early movies that shaped my ideas about male beauty and style. Tyrone Power, Errol Flynn, Clark Gable. This man fit the bill.

As I approached this dream figure with his classic graying beard and penetrating blue eyes, I read his name tag: Herb Kohler, Jr., President. Fastening my eyes on his, I extended my hand and introduced myself. "I'm Leda Sanford, publisher of *American Home*. I want to thank you, Mr. Kohler, for all the cooperation we received in developing the *American Home* bathroom for two. I hope you're as pleased as we are with the results. It has generated a lot of publicity."

"Oh, my dear, please call me Herb. May I call you Leda? Ah, Leda and the swan, one of my favorite myths."

We exchanged cards and pleasantries, and then Herb asked, "Can we have dinner next time I'm in New York?"

A smile crept across my face. "I'd be delighted."

I spent the rest of my time at the show thinking about him, and as I flew back to New York I replayed the meeting in my mind and fantasized about seeing him again.

Several weeks later his call came, and we arranged to meet at the Four Seasons. I was consumed with worries: What to wear? Where would this lead? What to tell Mort, who was not accustomed to my having dinner appointments?

I was still living with Mort, but I was tired of the relationship. Tired of his drinking and his need to believe that every woman he met wanted him. Although I was no longer in love with him, his cheating, real and imagined, still hurt. I wanted out but couldn't find the exit doors.

"I'm going out to dinner with an advertiser," I informed Mort as I dressed.

Mort rattled the ice in his glass of vodka and glared at me. "Okay, so who is this man? You usually don't go out to dinner with advertisers."

"Sorry, Mort, but I usually don't get to have dinner with the president of a company. It's usually lunch with a media director."

After deflecting a few more questions, I left the apartment and took a cab for the ten-block ride to Fifty-second Street. As I walked briskly up the marble steps leading to the Four Seasons, I paused to look at the Picasso tapestry hanging above the entrance. It always lifted my spirits.

"Good evening, Ms. Sanford," Julian, the maître d', greeted me warmly. "Your guest is here. Let me show you to your table."

The Four Seasons Pool Room was, and still is, one of New York's most dramatic settings for dining. The large pool in the center ringed by banquettes, the vaulted ceiling—it's a perfect backdrop for the aura of power that permeates the room.

Herb, rising to greet me, warmly took my hand and said, "I've been looking forward to this."

I scanned the room to see if there was anyone who might recognize me. No familiar faces.

Our dinner conversation focused on housing trends and Herb's latest invention, the Environment Masterbath, a large, futuristic cubicle that allowed the bather to experience wind, rain, and other conditions far beyond the traditional sauna or steam room. "There's an exterior panel where you can make your selections—any combination you'd like," Herb said. "Spring showers, jungle steam, tropical rain, and gentle breezes."

Herb clearly liked to create, invent, and challenge the status quo— an added attraction for me. His appetite for adventure came through, and soon we were talking more about ourselves and less about work.

After dessert, he asked if I knew of a nightclub we could go to.

"Of course. Let's go to Regine's."

Since Regine's was less than ten blocks away, we walked up Park Avenue, enjoying the brilliance of a New York night. Glittering skyscrapers rose up all around us, dominating symbols of the city's great wealth and power.

I love New York, I thought, *and I love being here, right now.*

Regine's dazzling décor, electric music, and undulating bodies of men and women dressed in designer fashions defined the tempo of a decade that both New Yorkers and Europeans agree was the best of times for the successful in Manhattan.

As Herb and I were led to a cocktail table, I could feel the vibrations between us intensify. Soon we were leaning toward one another sharing our mutual love of Emerson and Thoreau. In the midst of that pulsating, hedonistic setting, we were discussing our favorite philosophers. From there we moved on to our personal stories, mine set in Italy and New York, his in Wisconsin.

"When I was eighteen, I literally ran away with the circus that had come to our town," Herb confessed. "I didn't know what I was going to do, but I knew I didn't want to just work for a company and be in an office all day. But eventually I came back—there wasn't anything I could do in the circus. I never really wanted to go into the family business. Instead I wanted to be an actor. I really dislike business—hate the tedium, the numbers—and I'm bored by the kind of men who thrive on meetings."

We had inched closer and Herb slipped his hand under the back of my satin camisole, caressing my back.

I yearned to feel his arms around me.

"I want you," he breathed into my ear.

"And I want you too."

"Let's go," he whispered.

We took a cab to Herb's suite at the Carlyle Hotel. In contrast to Regine's, the Carlyle's traditional décor—damask, English mahogany—was staid and serious. *Well, I'm not going to let it dampen my emotions,* I thought as we embraced and tumbled as one onto the richly tufted comforter.

When I returned home late that night, Mort confronted me. "Where have you been? Isn't this rather late for a business dinner? Two AM."

His anger scared me. I didn't answer but moved quickly into the bathroom and shut the door. When I came out, he was already in bed, so I had no choice but to slide in as well. All night long I stayed as close to the edge as I could without falling out.

Next morning, the house phone rang and the concierge said a gentleman had just left a note for me. I asked that someone bring it up. The note was from Herb, with it an earring I'd lost in his room. In rather crude handwriting he thanked me for an unforgettable evening, signing it, simply, Herb.

Herb didn't know I was living with someone, because I hadn't told him. He obviously presumed I was single or he wouldn't have left a note. I knew he was married because he had shared some stories about his wife and family.

Mort was now standing beside me. "What's this?" he demanded, snatching the note from me. "Really? This is thanks for having dinner?"

Mort's rage was rising and with it my fear. Expletives poured forth, followed by threats: "You won't get away with this! Believe me, you're going to regret this. You're going to pay."

We were now standing on opposite sides of our queen-size bed, and I feared he might lunge at me. At that moment I knew I had to take control, that I had to get Mort out of my life. With or without Herb, I'd had enough; I wasn't going to wait for the physical violence all too common in domestic battles like this. I could recall vividly overhearing the quarrels between my mother and father in the night as I pulled the covers over my head and swore to God that no man would ever abuse me.

So as not to inflame Mort further, I said nothing.

I dressed for work and left quickly. At the office, I called my mother and shared my problem.

"You need a good matrimonial attorney," she said. "I'll ask Todd to locate one for you." Todd was my mother's husband. Although Mort and I weren't married, my mother thought an attorney would know how to extricate me from him safely.

Later that day Herb called wanting to know when we could meet again. I had decided seeing a married man didn't bother me. I'd already gotten used to it with Mort. Besides, it was the seventies.

"Where can we meet?" Herb asked with a flattering tone of urgency. I was scheduled to go to Chicago next, so we planned to meet at the Whitehall Hotel.

Anticipation is the greatest aphrodisiac. As I flew to Chicago, I immersed myself in recollections of the last time Herb and I were together and imagined what it would be like this time.

For many women, it is the desire to be desired that fuels their illicit episodes. For me it was more a reawakening of some part of myself, a part that had recently been furiously channeled into work.

Once together, we threw ourselves into each other's arms and made love. As we lay there blissfully, Herb smoking a cigar, there was a knock at the door.

"Who's there?" I asked.

"It's Mort," came the chilling reply.

"What are you doing here?" I asked, trembling.

"What are *you* doing here?" he countered.

"Go away or I'll call security," I answered.

"I know who you're with," he called, "and you are not going to get away with this."

Then he was gone. Somehow I wasn't afraid anymore. And Herb seemed only perplexed.

"Who was that?" he asked. "Why is he following you?"

I tried to dismiss it. "He's a man I was involved with who won't leave me alone."

"Hmm, very bad taste," Herb muttered. "I hope he's gone now."

With no second thought, we went back to our reason for being there.

* * *

Back in New York, I mustered my courage during the limo ride home. I knew what I had to tell Mort.

We fought behind our closed bedroom door, but the angry words reached my children listening in the other room.

"Mort, you have to leave. We can't go on living together. Please don't make this any worse than it already is. And lower your voice. The kids can hear us."

"Fuck the kids! You bitch! I left my family for you and now you're going to throw *me* out. No way. Not without a fight."

"Mort, it's over, and it's your fault, not mine. You and your drinking and your fooling around. I don't want you anymore."

I wouldn't let him get into bed with me, so he slept on the floor.

The next day I managed to pull myself together and go to work. First thing, I called the attorney my mother recommended. He provided an exit strategy that required a steely determination on my part: schedule a mover—my family's Santini Van Company would come in handy—and then pack up all of Mort's belongings in the presence of a witness. Have the belongings moved to a warehouse and change the locks on the doors to the apartment.

The attorney advised me to have two other adults present when Mort came home in the evening. I asked Todd Cole, my mother's husband and chairman of CIT Financial, and my ex, Howard, of all people. My sons were there as well.

When Mort returned home that evening, the doorman informed him that his suitcase was in the lobby and that the locks had been changed. Mort left but soon returned with two policemen who demanded entry because his name was on the lease.

The police ordered me to let him in. I refused. Then, as my attorney had advised, I issued a threat. While Howard, Todd, and my children watched in horror, I shouted through the door, "If you make me let him in, I'll kill him!"

"No, ma'am," the police officer implored. "You don't mean that."

"Yes I do—and I have the knife here to do it."

By law, the police are obliged to prevent a crime, and my threat forced them to prevent Mort from entering.

Todd offered to put Mort up at the nearby Mayfair Regent Hotel, but Mort refused and finally stormed off.

I was awakened the following morning by a phone call from Todd. He asked me to sit down as he proceeded to read a headline from the *New York Daily News*: "*American Home* publisher throws lover out of East Side apartment." The story claimed I had tossed Mort's clothes out of the nineteenth-floor window because I was having an affair with Herb Kohler, the plumbing magnate.

I slumped in my chair. How had the papers gotten this? Ah, Mort's journalistic connections. Probably his old comrade, Jim Brady, the columnist at the *Daily News*.

Dazed and confused, I somehow got myself dressed and to the office. It took all the will power I could muster not to let this scandal unravel me. My face never betrayed my roiling emotions as I walked into my office, attended to my staff, and held a circulation meeting.

No one said anything about the news, but their expressions were cold and hard as they waited for me to call the meeting to order. When I greeted them and asked, "Are there any questions regarding the news of the day?" no one smiled. Carlo, I noted, did not jump to my defense or try to defrost the air. He sat stiffly in his Ivy League suit, button-down collar, and crew-cut hair, a frigid expression on his face.

Not till much later did I realize how much I threatened Carlo's male ego, as well as his place on the ladder of succession at Charter. I had learned through the grapevine how adept he was at managing lower-echelon women, most of whom thought he was sexy. He favored the youngest and prettiest staffers with a regard he did not bestow on older women. But no one seemed to know for sure if he actually had interoffice affairs. If so, he'd been spared the embarrassment I was facing now.

The next few weeks were filled with meetings with lawyers amid more newspaper articles about the scandalous publisher of *American Home*. Herb, through his lawyers, denied everything. He was in China, on a trade mission with the governor of Minnesota.

What did I expect from him? Not much really. I quickly realized that our affair did not justify his jeopardizing his family or reputation. We hadn't had time to move beyond the insanely passionate stage into real bonding, where loyalty is born. Our reputations were being jeopardized by the ghoulish press, so naturally we tried to protect ourselves with denials. Intellectually I knew this, but in my heart I was hoping he would reach out to me and express some concern. For a long time, whenever the phone rang, I hoped it would be him simply asking, "How are you?"

That call never came.

7. Ecco l'America

My indiscretion seemed like a footnote compared to the larger events shaking up the Charter empire. Charter's fortune was strongly tied to foreign oil. No other publishing company was so beholden to a single aspect of our economy. Perhaps this overriding concern caused Mason to minimize the importance of the media attention my scandalous behavior was causing in New York. It was almost irrelevant.

The positive gains that Charter Publishing was making (by now the largest publishing conglomerate in the United States) and the acceptance that *American Home* was achieving in the marketplace were overshadowed by the intense activities revolving around Mason's efforts to expand. There were cost overruns at their Houston refinery, and former New York Governor Hugh Carey was working with Mason to structure a merger with Carey Energy, a goal achieved in 1979.

Mason's investment in the magazine business was a trivial pursuit compared to the scope of his involvement with Middle Eastern kings and political heavyweights. At its peak, Charter was an organization of 180 subsidiaries. In 1975, the year I visited Epping Forest, Egyptian President Anwar Sadat had met there with Vice President Gerald Ford. President Richard Nixon, his first choice, had been unavailable due to Watergate. Flags of the two nations on giant adjacent flagpoles were flapping in the wind behind Mason's mansion—part of preparations for Sadat's arrival.

Sadly, in the fall of 1977, just as *American Home* was turning the financial corner, I was advised that the December issue would be the last and that the publication would be merged with *Redbook* for greater operating efficiency. The closing of *American Home* had been rumored "on the street," but Carlo had denied it until the day he arrived at my office, shut the door, and with no delicacy confirmed that rumor and Charter's decision to consolidate their publishing activities.

He offered no words of consolation and made no effort to soften the blow. Wearing his characteristic steely expression, he explained that I would receive a handsome severance package, one year's salary, benefits, and a letter of recommendation.

There was no point in asking for a little more time. Like a death sentence, it had been pronounced.

Holding back tears was the best I could do. We shook hands and I watched him walk stiffly out the door. At that moment, I hated him as I have seldom hated anyone. I knew that he had never provided the help he was supposed to and probably had been secretly hoping I would fail. My failure validated the male chauvinism he lived by.

The headlines in the industry publications announcing the closing of *American Home* in 1978 were merciless. It was as if the trade journals and newsletters, which existed to support publishing and advertising, were taking particular pleasure in the fall of *this* particular magazine. Were they motivated by the perverse thrill of watching the failure of the idea behind the magazine — that women should question their traditional lifestyles? After all, *American Home* had challenged the women's home service magazine formula for financial success.

Or was it my fault?

I was the rebel with a cause who had not been able to gain the support of the advertising decision makers. Among them were agency executives, whose anxiety about losing clients prevented them from altering their marketing paradigm. Pundits had predicted the futility of suggesting that marketing strategies, which had worked for years, should be altered to accommodate a new woman.

Advertising agencies who served clients like Proctor and Gamble and General Foods were not interested in doing the additional work and research required to convince their clients of a new approach and perhaps jeopardize their relationships with prized accounts. They understood the traditional woman and how to push her buttons. That was enough.

Next I had to face the painful duty of firing sixty or so employees at Christmas time.

I scheduled meetings with the managers, who in turn would discharge the people who reported to them. Although I had fired many employees in recent years, they were usually underperformers, and my dissatisfaction justified my action and tempered any emotional pain.

But this was different. These were loyal, enthusiastic people, who were now in shock. With a firm handshake, and sometimes a warm hug, I told them that while I did not know where I would go next, they should feel free to contact me when I was settled. In a few cases I had to fight back tears. Usually they hugged me back, to reassure me that yes, things would be all right.

Although I had occasionally wondered what would happen if my career collapsed, if I stumbled in the competitive rat race, I was neither financially nor psychologically prepared for the actual moment.

Ensconced in the same leather chair I had claimed eagerly almost three years before, I now felt small and powerless, like Alice after she drank the potion. I stared out the corner window, looking down light-studded Fifty-second Street as it stretched toward the west side of Manhattan. Watching the traffic lights shimmering in the distance, I shuddered involuntarily.

Who am I now? I thought. No job, no title. Lacking those, I was just a woman without an identity.

I opened the top drawer of my desk and began to empty the contents into my briefcase. Spotting my passport, I opened it to the picture. There I was, forced smile, face framed by short curly hair. I read the information as if for the first time: Date of birth: October 11, 1933. Place of birth: Italy.

I glanced up, looking west toward the Hudson River piers, where I'd often watched giant ocean liners dock, and one of my earliest memories surfaced—the beginning of my life in the United States.

It was May 1939, and I was five and a half years old. My father was holding me as high as he could on the deck of the *Rex,* one of Italy's premier ocean liners. Pointing to the Statue of Liberty, he said, *"Ecco, l'America. Ecco, l'America."*

The ship was filled with tourists and some Europeans who, like my family, were fleeing because of the threat of war. My father, Fausto Giovannetti, an enthusiastic follower of Mussolini, had not wanted to leave Italy. He acceded only after insistent messages from my grandparents in New York and pleadings from my mother that we escape Europe before a war started.

Waiting for us at the New York pier, standing next to a shiny black Packard, were Aunt Dora and my grandparents, who had immigrated to the United States in 1918. Grandpa, I'd been told, had realized his dream of a better life in America. He owned a moving and storage company.

Much to Grandpa's dismay, my mother had married an Italian and gone back to the very place they had fled. Only today, as a grandparent, can I fully comprehend what happiness and relief they must have felt as they embraced me and my baby sister, Paola.

We didn't have much luggage since my father believed we would be returning to Europe in a few months. Not knowing that, my grandfather had brought one of his moving vans to transport our belongings.

The Santini Van Company truck was imposing and somewhat ludicrous as two moving men placed our few suitcases into the cavernous truck. Then we all piled into the shiny, black Packard and drove up the West Side Highway to 928 Morris Park Avenue in the Bronx, where excited neighbors were standing by to welcome us.

After the truck was unpacked, my grandfather informed the family that he was going to take me for a ride. No explanations.

We drove to Third Avenue and then under the elevated-train trestle to Cornell's, a legendary specialty children's store, where Grandpa bought me a blue organdy dress. I felt like a little princess in a fairy tale.

At first I couldn't speak English, but by September, when I was enrolled in Our Lady of Solace, I was nearly fluent. This, in spite of my father's determination that I not forget Italian. He even imposed a rule that only Italian would be spoken at the dinner table.

I don't know why I wanted to be American, but I did. Even at a young age, I resisted the pressure to conform to my Italian family's values. For weeks at a time, I expressed my defiance by refusing to speak at all. If I wanted salt, I would point to it.

Later, as I was allowed to speak English, a result of my mother's insistence, I began to share at the dinner table what I had learned at Catholic school. I was attending parochial school because at that time in the Bronx, only the poor went to public schools. My father, a basic anticlerical Italian Catholic, would ridicule me for believing the nonsense the nuns were pedaling about saints and miracles. Most of his snide comments were directed at priests and nuns.

"It's their job to keep you ignorant. They want to scare you with superstition and tales of miracles. Don't you believe a word of it."

"But ... but," I would interject, "Sister Mary Francis said—"

"*Piccola sapiente*," Fausto would interrupt sharply. It meant "little know-it-all," and it was his put-down nickname for me.

In that environment, I eventually learned to stand up for myself not so much by talking back but by not crying. There was no arguing with my father. As for my grandfather, he did not rail against the Catholic Church. He had turned against the church after his thirteen-year-old son died. He never set foot in a church again except for weddings and funerals.

Now, as I leaned back in the voluminous chair I'd inherited from John Mack Carter (I would miss that chair!), I knew that if I were to survive this potentially crushing defeat, I would have to summon not just wisdom and smarts—all I knew or thought I knew—but also the basic courage I had developed as a child. More than survive—I had to rebuild!

I walked over to my office closet and slipped into my lynx fur coat, the most visible expression of my success. It enveloped me in a luxury I had grown all too accustomed to. I cherished it as much as any of the material things I'd acquired in this second life.

I held it tightly around myself, took one last look around my pretentious office, and walked out of the Charter building and into a light snow that had begun to fall. The corporate limousine was parked outside, and James, the driver, rolled down the window and called out a friendly, "Hi, Merry Christmas, Ms. Sanford. Need a lift?"

"Merry Christmas, James," I said numbly. "No thanks."

Although it was snowing, I decided to walk up Lexington Avenue toward home. Wrapping my wool muffler over my head, I felt that refreshing feeling that nature can provide even in the urban canyons of Manhattan.

Visions of past Christmases flashed through my mind, of holidays that revolved around family and beloved traditions.

I saw myself in that other role, my first life, wearing a red sweater, plaid skirt, and holiday apron, my hair in a fifties' flip. I was moving efficiently about our cozy colonial home, putting things in order, setting the dining room table with meticulous care. Yes, that house on Linden Avenue was the picture-perfect American home.

My thoughts were interrupted. I was nearing Sixty-fifth Street and my present home.

The Phoenix, my thirty-two-story concrete high-rise, was a far cry from the white Colonial house in the suburbs that I'd left behind seven years before. The dramatic, long front canopy stenciled with the building's name that extended from the revolving front door to the street was capped with snow.

I greeted Tommy, the uniformed doorman, went through the revolving door, and entered the expansive marble lobby. The opulence always gave me a sense of importance, but this time that feeling was quickly tempered by the cold wind of reality: I was unemployed.

I tapped my feet to shake off the snow and then entered the elevator and pushed the button for the nineteenth floor. It felt good to be home, to know that someone I loved was waiting there for me. The jangle of my keys as I groped for the keyhole signaled my arrival, and Scott, my fifteen-year-old son, opened the door.

"Mom!"

His handsome smile, the emotional punch of that single syllable—it was my reality check, bringing me back, as it always did, to the center of my life, to what really counted.

"Mom, are you okay?"

"No," I blurted, the words collapsing into tears.

Scott was now taller than me, but his face, framed by curly blond hair, was as cherubic as when he was two. He reminded me of a guardian angel in a medieval fresco.

"It's okay, Mom. It's okay." He kept repeating this, like some religious litany.

I collapsed onto the couch, and Scott stood over me, his hand resting gently on my shoulder. He had never seen me cry. He had rarely seen me down. I was always the strong one, the model of courage and strength. He probably believed that nothing could break my spirit and that I would always be there for him and for Robert, guiding their lives, making them proud because I "wasn't an ordinary mother."

What would happen to them now? How would this change their lives? What about the luxurious apartment they called home, the private schools they attended? The meager support their father provided would never be enough. Suddenly the lifestyle I had constructed so rapidly and so audaciously was hanging in the balance.

"Thanks, Scott. I'm all right. I'll change and then we can talk over dinner."

My forest-green bedroom with mirrored walls and white Angelo Donghia furniture had always boosted my spirits. The New York skyline framed by the corner windows never ceased to thrill me. It was the view I had often fantasized about as a teenager.

As I removed my suit and changed into velour lounging pajamas, I watched the light blinking on and off atop the Empire State Building. Its needlelike tip was all I could see anymore. The rest of its 102 stories were blocked by the skyline that had sprung up in the midseventies, watered by the real estate boom.

I sat in one of my plush white armchairs and stared out at the city lights. This apartment, this view, this home—all part of a dream realized, a goal achieved. I had spent many happy hours reveling in its comfort and beauty. It represented the lifestyle I had always wanted.

My briefcase, which I had dropped against a chair leg, fell over with a thud, interrupting my thoughts. Then the phone rang.

It was René d'Auriac, an art director and an old friend.

"Hello, Leda, this is René. I heard what happened. So sorry. What a blow."

"Thanks, René," I said with no enthusiasm.

"Guess what?" he said excitedly. "I'm working on an unusual magazine. We're in crisis and need a publisher/editor immediately. Do you want to hear about it?"

Was he kidding? I dreaded the thought of looking for another job, of having to sell myself while disassociating myself from the *American Home* failure. I shuddered at the thought of trying to explain why the closure of *American Home* had not been my fault.

"What magazine?" I asked.

"It's called *Chief Executive*. You've probably never heard of it because it's very exclusive, available only to twenty-five thousand chief executives, who must meet certain criteria for qualification."

"I don't have any experience in the business magazine field," I replied.

"It doesn't matter, Leda. The concept is based on inviting chief executives and heads of state to write the articles. They get assurance they won't be edited. The advertising is really payback from the companies whose CEOs are featured. It's pure quid pro quo."

"Well, René, that's a departure from always trying to protect a magazine's editorial integrity," I replied.

"Think about it. At least meet the owner. He's an original. Call tomorrow and set up a time. It's urgent. If they don't publish the next issue, the magazine will have to fold."

I thought about it: *Maybe René's offer was a lifeline.* After all, there were few openings at the top of the magazine field, and my reputation as a challenger of the status quo would not make me appealing to staid organizations like Hearst, Condé Nast, and Meredith.

Why not at least meet the owner?

8. Chief Executive

In early January of 1978, I met John Deuss, the chairman of Joc Oil and the publisher of *Chief Executive* magazine. My appointment was for 6:00 p.m. at the Olympic Tower at 645 Fifth Avenue, standing majestically on the northeast corner of Fifty-first Street. The Olympic Tower was the newest and most dazzling skyscraper built in recent years. Only six blocks from the offices of *American Home* on Lexington Avenue, it was as opulent as our office building was austere.

As I walked through the revolving door and into the glistening marble lobby, with a waterfall in full cascade, the uniformed doorman directed me to the polished brass desk and the sign-in book. After passing through security, I was allowed to take the elevator to the nineteenth floor.

The building had replaced the white marble twelve-story Best & Co. department store, where I had experienced some of my happiest shopping moments as a teen. Until the completion of the Trump Tower many years later, the Olympic Tower had the highest profile of any building on Fifth Avenue. The project had originally targeted buyers from Europe and the Middle East, and the developer was owned by a family trust of famed international mogul Aristotle Onassis (thus the name Olympic, after Olympic Airways, which Onassis owned).

The glass double door to the Joc Oil company and the offices of *Chief Executive* opened automatically as I approached. I was feeling apprehensive about this meeting I'd had the audacity to accept. As with my first meeting with Raymond K. Mason, I knew nothing about the man I was about to meet. There wasn't Google to come to my rescue.

"I'm here to see Mr. Deuss. I'm Leda Sanford. I have a six o'clock appointment."

"I'll announce you, Ms. Sanford," the receptionist replied. "Make yourself comfortable."

I sat in one of the chairs that formed a semicircle around a table upon which were carefully arranged copies of *Chief Executive* magazine and an annual report for Joc Oil.

"He's ready to see you now, Ms. Sanford," the receptionist announced, and with a "follow me," she led me into the executive suite.

As I approached Deuss, who was seated behind a mammoth desk, I felt as if I were on a stage. It was dusk, and the spires of St. Patrick's Cathedral were silhouetted in the floor-to-ceiling windows behind him. He appeared sinister at first, with his Hitleresque hairdo. But as he stood, smiled, and extended his hand to welcome me, I was immediately charmed. Power enhances the male persona, and Deuss exuded power. I had already discovered that, and, oddly, that it does not apply equally to women.

"Ms. Sanford," Deuss began, "may I call you Leda?"

"Of course," I replied, handing him my résumé. My heart raced and my hands trembled.

He scanned it quickly and then replied, "Well, Raymond K. Mason? Hmm, a fellow oil man. If you worked for him for three and a half years, that's good enough for me."

What a stroke of luck, I thought.

Then he continued: "This is a very ugly situation. I hope you have the stomach for it, as well as the publishing expertise. And it must be resolved quickly. We must publish the next issue of *Chief Executive* on time or else our legitimate right to this franchise will be challenged.

"Here's the background: Several years ago I met a man named Henry O. Dormann in the lobby of a hotel in Kenya. A few drinks later, we had concocted the idea of creating a magazine written for and by chief executives and leaders, who all believe the press is controlled by liberal elitists. What we decided to do was invite CEOs and presidents of major companies to write for the magazine with the assurance that we would not edit their articles except for grammar. We would offer them a platform for their unedited opinions. You understand, right?"

I nodded and nervously asked, "Who will provide the advertising support to finance the magazine? That's especially important if it's to be distributed free to the qualified."

"I intend to fund it. Any advertising revenue is a plus. The benefit for me is that I gain access to many influential leaders who are crucial to my business success.

"My agreement with Dormann was, I would provide the capital and he would manage the magazine and do all the entertaining required."

Deuss leaned closer, as if in confidence. "Frankly, Leda, and this is not to leave this room, Dormann abused the power and freedom I gave him. He maintained an extravagant lifestyle at my expense. Would you like to see the marble bathroom he had installed in his office? The day he came to me and showed me the sterling-silver coffee service he had bought for the office ... I fired him.

"Then I left for a trip abroad. When I returned to New York, I found the offices of *Chief Executive* had been stripped of all magazine contents, and Dormann had advised advertisers that the magazine was now called *Leaders* and was owned and operated by Dormann at 59 East Fifty-fourth Street. All advertising materials were to be sent to that address."

As my eyes widened at this tale of intrigue and double-dealing, Deuss looked at me with steely eyes and said, "Do you think you can do this? The only editorial material we have in-house is an interview I conducted with Ian Smith, the new prime minister of Rhodesia. I want him on the cover."

"Absolutely," I replied.

"Well then, let's discuss terms and salary."

"My fee is ten thousand a month. I'd also like complete freedom to hire the necessary staff and a modest expense account for entertaining and travel. For operating, I will need an art director and a managing editor to manage production. I'll submit a budget."

Deuss stood up abruptly, smiled, and said, "Fine, when can you start? I will need to see a budget immediately."

"I can start tomorrow. And I'll have the budget ready on Monday," I said, extending my hand.

As I exited through the revolving gold doors of the Tower and onto Fifth Avenue, my feet barely touched the pavement. For now, I could hardly wait to tell my mother and children how I had landed a new job in less than a week, how I'd snatched victory from the jaws of defeat. I couldn't help thinking of Scarlet O'Hara in the last scene of *Gone with the Wind*. Yes, I would think about it tomorrow—the hard stuff, that is. In the meantime, our worries were over, or so I thought.

My mother, always my biggest supporter, was thrilled and, she added, not surprised. Her husband, Todd, was. Knowing that my talents lay in writing and design, he wondered aloud how I would manage in such a highly charged, financially oriented setting. He was familiar with the magazine.

For Scott and Robert, it was another act in the unfolding drama of my life. They had learned to adapt.

Mort, on the other hand, was slow to adapt. My ability to maintain the lifestyle I had created in Manhattan had also been jeopardized by Mort's unrelenting efforts to get revenge. At one point I had to obtain a restraining order to keep him far from me and my sons, because in an effort to be closer to me he had tried to rent an apartment in our building.

Why couldn't he let go? Why wouldn't he give up? The legal costs had eroded my savings ...

Back home on the nineteenth floor of the Phoenix, I felt that I had been rescued from the edge. Gazing out at the glittering Manhattan skyline, I thought, *What a perfect setting for a romantic liaison*. When, I wondered, would that happen? For now it was my eagle's nest, my haven, and tonight I felt special joy knowing that it was mine and not in jeopardy.

The next day, after being shown around the magazine's offices, I began my search for an art director. I had someone in mind, a man I'd long admired and who was now out of work. Paul Hardy had been the art director of *Working Woman* but left when the magazine was sold. I found his number and called him. We made an appointment to meet.

"The Olympic Tower?" Paul asked. "Wow, that's impressive. Not the usual setting for a start-up."

Paul became the art director of *Chief Executive* magazine as well as my longtime artistic soul mate. The fourth issue of *CEM* was published on time. John Deuss was ecstatic and Dormann was not. My ability to convince the few advertisers who had committed to the issue to honor their contracts reflected my relationship with people like Constantine Kazanes at Young & Rubican. I relied on people who knew and trusted me, despite the *American Home* debacle.

One evening, Deuss took the staff to Regine's to celebrate, lavishing praise on us for our fine work. Smiling and exuberant in the shimmering light of the night club, Deuss looked remarkably attractive.

9. The Joy of Money

Although the leap from home-service subjects in *American Home* to the arena of world affairs and high finance was a stretch for me, 1978 became my year of living extravagantly and a little dangerously.

I planned a luxury trip to Italy and splurged on some splendid luxury goods that I still enjoy today. A full set of Gucci luggage and Ferragamo shoes softened the lingering sting of emotional loss. Bouquets of fresh flowers in my home fulfilled a lifelong desire. With a year of severance pay from Charter and my new salary from Joc Oil, I finally had financial peace of mind.

But Mort continued to lurk in the background of my mind, a paranoia of sorts that surfaced whenever I attended a gala event in Manhattan where he might turn up. Because he had moved to East Sixty-eighth Street, a mere two blocks from the Phoenix, I was cautious about which streets I walked, my eyes darting about on the chance that he might be there. Seeing him would revive conflicting feelings that would roil my soul. Would he be with another woman? Would I feel jealousy? Did I still care? In spite of all the pain he had caused, there was still an undeniable attraction.

When I wasn't working, I concentrated on my son Scott, now sixteen. That summer we took a first-class trip to Italy, starting in Rome with a suite at the fabled Hassler Hotel. Scott, awestruck by the Coliseum and Roman Forum, impetuously embraced an ancient column, exclaiming, "I can't believe I'm here!"

From Rome we drove to Tuscany to visit my father in Pievefosciana, in the province of Lucca. Only the photos I have confirm that this meeting ever happened, because in my memory it remains surrealistic. In the medieval town where he lived and I'd been born, nothing had changed. Fausto, my father, had aged only slightly since the last time I'd seen him in 1973. He was still the distant unemotional figure that had always cast a shadow over my life. In spite of this, I was proud of him because he was a talented painter and writer and profoundly intellectual. My positive feelings for Italy and the Italian people were resurrected, as well as my dislike for the Catholic Church.

Back in the expansive Manhattan offices of *Chief Executive*, I worked in relative peace with my small staff in our wing of the nineteenth floor. Meanwhile, in adjacent offices the sound of oil traders shouting prices rose above the din of clattering teletype machines.

One of the key elements in executing my vision for this particular magazine was the graphic design, which was realized by Paul Hardy, the most talented art director I ever worked with. He had an exquisite sensibility regarding type and graphics, and the spring 1978 issue of *Chief Executive* magazine with Ian Smith, prime minister of Rhodesia, on the cover and dramatic layouts within exemplifies this. He also contributed his talent to help me produce an annual report for the first Curacao International Bank, which Deuss had founded. It was disturbing working with numbers that seemed of undocumented origin, but it was fascinating to watch how design and graphics lent credibility to the fictitious contents. As I look at what we produced today, I am filled with admiration for Paul's talent. I miss him. He died too young in 2001.

Although I was enjoying my elevated status as publisher of *Chief Executive*, I occasionally heard things that made me uncomfortable. One time I passed an open doorway and heard, in a foreign accent punctuated by a tone of urgency, this nebulous wisp of conversation:

"So raise the offer ... the son-of-a-bitch ... no more options ... won't be pretty ... where is the tanker now?"

Although I couldn't make sense of it, I knew this was no executive-speak. My growing sense of unease made me open to leaving *Chief Executive* as soon as I could find a way. To the end, however, I was treated with respect.

Years later, when John Deuss was arrested, investigations into his activities revealed foreign intrigue that should be fodder for a dramatic book. Deuss was at the center of a corporate and espionage spiderweb that linked him directly to a man named Ted Shackley—the infamous Blond Ghost—who organized shipments of oil to South Africa, then under a global embargo that Deuss cheerfully flouted. The Internet is rich with shady background material on Deuss, waiting for an author to assemble it all.

When Deuss summoned me to his office one day to review the upcoming editorial plan, I was surprised to hear him say that he wanted to interview the prime minister of Italy, Giulio Andreotti.

"Well, Leda, do you think you can obtain that meeting for me?"

"It's possible, John," I replied. "I have some excellent connections here in New York in the Italian community. The Italian Trade Commissioner, Lucio Caputo, lives at the Phoenix, and I know him well. I'll do my best."

This was a turbulent time in Italy, which was under siege from the Red Brigades. Much of their terrorism targeted CEOs. Nevertheless, with surprising ease I managed to arrange the interview, achieving a scoop, something even the mainstream press hadn't been able to accomplish.

In the course of investigating the Italian scene, I learned about Jeno Paulucci, one of America's richest men and a colorful entrepreneur who had started the Chun King Corporation, the Chinese food company, and then sold it to R.J. Reynolds. After that he started Jeno's, Inc., which today has morphed into Michelina's frozen entrees, named after his mother.

I also learned that Jeno had started the Italian American Foundation in Washington and was now on the verge of starting a magazine for Italian Americans.

I knew I had to meet this man and convince him to make me his editor-in-chief. The mere thought of spearheading the creation of a magazine for and about Italians excited me and filled me with a sense of mission and purpose for a cause I could embrace. Two other attempts to start a magazine for Italian Americans had flopped, largely because the owners knew nothing about publishing. In my opinion those magazines had been tacky and amateurish, like many ethnic publications of the time. They certainly were not reflective of the Italian reputation for fine design and superlative artistic achievement. If anything, they perpetuated the stereotypes that haunted Italian Americans and made so many distance themselves from their heritage. Most of the images used in advertising and in the movies depicted Italian American men either as low-class gangsters, *mafiosi*, or simply uneducated proprietors of pizza parlors. Fat Italian women stirring tomato sauce over a hot stove competed with Sophia Loren, the sexy seductress, as role models for Italian American women.

I felt strongly that the challenge of creating a magazine that would be a source of genuine pride for Italian Americans required someone who saw the danger inherent in creating a chauvinistic publication that would be labeled ethnic. That positioning would narrow the appeal to both subscribers and advertisers and doom it to failure.

I wrote a brief letter to Jeno. No long-winded pitch. Simply, I want to meet you and tell you why you should put me in charge of this project.

The phone rang early one morning a week later. The caller wasted no words. "This is Jeno Paulucci. I'll be in Washington this week. Can you meet me at the Hay Adams for breakfast on Wednesday at eight thirty?"

Without hesitation I said yes. No questions asked. What I'd learned from my prior bosses was that quick-thinking entrepreneurs want fast responses and want to be spared the details. In fact, Jeno admitted later that mine was the shortest letter he ever received and that he liked that.

I made a reservation at the Hay Adams and caught a train to Washington. As I walked into the dining room, I recognized Jeno from his pictures. He was sitting with his assistant, Joe Nardi. Strangely, I wasn't nervous, although my investigation into Jeno Paulucci's background had revealed that he had little patience and could be brutal in his dealings with people.

"He'll eat you alive," one former associate warned me.

"He's a killer," said another.

"He's brilliant but surrounds himself with mediocre people who play to his ego. He's never put a woman in any position of authority."

Somehow all those negatives only made me feel more excited about meeting Jeno Paulucci.

"Mr. Paulucci, good morning. Hope I didn't keep you waiting."

"Nope. This is my assistant, Joe Nardi. Have a seat. Waiter, we're ready."

No time for menu scanning. Clearly, Jeno was ready to order and presumed that everyone else was too. Besides, who needed a menu for breakfast?

I ordered a slice of melon and coffee, Jeno ordered iced tea, and Joe ordered orange juice, bacon and eggs, toast and coffee, ample evidence that he did not plan to talk much.

With no warm-up, Jeno launched into his plan to publish a magazine for Italian Americans. With shining eyes and an unflinching expression that seemed to convey both anger and pride, he recounted the story of his childhood in Milwaukee. How he had suffered abuse and discrimination because he was a "wop." How, even now, years later and with a net worth of $800 million, he suspected that many of his highly placed political and corporate friends still thought he was "connected."

He went on to tell me how he had visited Italy for the first time when he was forty years old and that he had been overcome with pride and surprise at the legacy that was his. He'd had no time for culture since he had started foraging for a living on the streets of Milwaukee. He continued talking, hammering away at his main points, criticizing a biased press, television stereotypes, and the advertising world for capitalizing on prejudice and misbeliefs.

I listened and nodded periodically. I understood his sentiments and identified with his dream. But I also understood that the challenge of publishing was only complicated by worthy causes. And the kind of power and influence with the public that Jeno was looking for was the province of newspapers. Of course, I wasn't going to tell him this.

Then Jeno really got down to business. He had, he said, bought the subscriber lists of the two now-defunct magazines *I Am* and *Identity* when their assets had been auctioned off. He believed this gave him a leg up in the critical area of subscription sales. He said he'd been on the verge of hiring the former editor of *I Am*, Ron Depaolo, for this magazine. That is, until he received my letter.

He wanted to call the magazine *Attenzione* because he had seen this word all over Italy, where it is a common road sign. It simply means attention, watch out!

"I don't care whether you like that or not—I like it," he said, with no provocation.

Well, I thought, *concessions must be made. Besides, magazine titles are always a gamble.* Although I didn't like it, I wasn't going to get hung up on the name, and I wasn't going to start my relationship with this notoriously dictatorial man by arguing with him about it. I knew from experience that the name of a magazine means nothing until the magazine exists and imposes meaning on it.

When it was my turn, I offered, with appropriate passion, my theories about what I saw as a new demographic—upwardly mobile Americans of Italian origin—and how desperately they needed a publication that would reinforce their self-esteem and give them a sense of justifiable pride, not chauvinism.

Stereotyping Italians as gangsters or loud, spaghetti-eating blue-collar types was still common. In response, many ambitious Italian Americans were changing their names in an attempt to conceal their ethnicity and increase their chances of climbing the ladder of success. Jeno himself had changed his name from Gino Paolucci to Jeno Paulucci in a youthful attempt to disguise his background.

Because I was Italian born, had been an immigrant, and clearly had fire in my belly, I was his ideal spokesperson and director of this campaign. I told Jeno that in order to achieve the objective of raising the image of Italian Americans, this magazine had to be first class, on par with the best magazines in the field.

Earlier ethnic publications had been notoriously downscale, not only editorially but in terms of the advertising they attracted.

Jeno understood what I was saying and seemed to agree.

He informed me that he wanted to launch the magazine by July 1979, giving me only six months to hire the entire staff and create a publication with advertising. Could I do that?

"Could you submit a business plan so we could get started?"

"Certainly."

"Good. I'd like to see it by January."

That was it. We shook hands and said good-bye, and only then did I realize that neither of us had eaten breakfast. Over the years I discovered that the movers and shakers rarely do. It's just a setting for transacting business.

Back in New York, I bravely gave John Deuss my resignation. He wished me well, thanked me for having saved the magazine, and with a bear hug said good-bye. I was a blip on the screen of his momentous life.

I had hired a capable young man, J. P. Donlon, as editor, so there would be no missed steps except maybe in advertising sales. J. P. had worked for me at *Men's Wear*, and he seemed to me a perfect fit for this environment. Indeed he was, for twenty-five years later he is still with the publication, having survived several buyouts and mergers.

I wrote the business plan for *Attenzione* in December, enlisting the circulation and list-management expertise of Paul Goldberg, who later became my circulation mentor.

The plan was sent to Jeno, and the first week in January he called and asked me to come to Duluth, the company headquarters, to meet with him. He said he liked the numbers and the strategy. Arrangements had been made for me to fly to Minneapolis, stay overnight, and then take a commuter plane to Duluth the next morning.

Dressed in fur-lined boots, fur coat, fur hat, fur-lined gloves, and wool muffler, I disembarked from the plane into a frozen, snow-covered landscape reminiscent of *Dr. Zhivago*. A car and driver were waiting for me, and I was driven directly to the offices of Jeno's, Inc., a dreary factory building on the outskirts of the city.

Jeno was waiting in the conference room, flanked by Joe Nardi and another executive. I again marveled at my self-assurance.

After the briefest of preliminaries, Jeno said, "The plan looks reasonable. Now, what do you want as compensation?"

"Eighty thousand a year and first-class travel, including a limousine," I replied unflinchingly.

My instinct told me that the hundred and twenty grand I'd been making would not sit well with Jeno. I was guessing the man he'd been considering had probably asked for forty thousand.

"First-class travel?" Jeno repeated. "Well, you certainly know how to live. Okay. Done."

A smile crept over my face.

"Now," he said, "we have office space on Times Square. Look the space over and let me know what you think. If you think the offices aren't suitable, you can find others. Also, I'd like you to fly down to

Peewaukee to meet with Larry Quadracci. He has a printing plant there, and I'd like him to be the printer. Joe will fly down with you in one of our planes. Let me know what you think of Larry's operation."

With a handshake and a pat on the back from Jeno, I was off to the airport.

No sooner were we in the air than a snowstorm engulfed us, tossing the plane about like a rag doll. Shaken, I finally made it to the Milwaukee airport, where Larry Quadracci and a snowplow met me.

Quadracci, in 1979, was mostly a printer of "skin" books, as some called *Playboy* and the like. Adding *Attenzione* to his stable of magazines helped legitimize Larry's company, and over time it became a multimillion-dollar business.

My trip to Quad Graphics was a formality, I later realized. It really didn't matter what I thought, as the deal with Quadracci had already been cut.

With that visit, I headed back to New York to start *Attenzione.*

10. La Dolce Vita ... for a while

The seedy office near Times Square that Joe Nardi had located as headquarters for *Attenzione* was a far cry from the Olympic Tower.

In a dreary and minor building on a side street, the four-room office was reached by walking down a gray hallway flanked by offices with fogged glass doors featuring company names. Night and Day Frocks and Schwartz Buttons reflected our location on the fringe of the garment district.

The few metal desks and chairs left behind by the former occupant allowed us to begin work. But the place contradicted our company's stated purpose—"to promote a new and elevated image of Italian Americans"—and I knew I'd have trouble persuading people to work in such an environment, including myself.

Mustering my courage, I confronted Jeno and asked for permission to locate a more suitable address. He agreed.

Remarkably, I was able to locate ten thousand square feet of space on Forty-ninth Street between Fifth and Madison Avenues, directly across from Saks Fifth Avenue. With little time to spare, I directed renovation of the space while interviewing candidates for the staff jobs and hiring my choices. There was no time for vacillation—the launch date for *Attenzione* was July, six months away.

Already there were grumblings in the Italian American community because I wasn't hiring Italian Americans, and Jeno fed some of the complaints back to me.

"Hey, Leda," he bellowed into the phone. "What's the matter? You can't find some people with Italian American names to put in the magazine? And by the way, you'll have to use your Italian name. It'll help me defend my choice of you as publisher and editor."

When I said nothing, his voice rose another few decibels: "Okay? Leda Giovannetti—got it?"

So I would have to use my family name again. I'd become Leda Sanford. That's how everyone knew me. "Jeno," I said haltingly. "It would be a mistake for me to drop Sanford because that's how I'm known in the business. Can we compromise on Leda Giovannetti Sanford?"

"Awright, you have a point," he growled.

Anxious to change the subject, I said, "Jeno, by the way, I am going to hire the most qualified people in New York, only those I feel have the sensibility required to execute this challenging concept. They may not all have Italian names."

I was glad he wasn't in the room to see my hands trembling.

"Do you understand what I mean, Jeno? It won't be easy to create an award-winning magazine that doesn't look like a promotion for the Italian travel industry or Italian wines. We have to replace tired stereotypes with a more nuanced reality."

I pressed on, hoping Jeno was nodding in agreement. "We need a staff of talented people with no personal motive—regardless of nationality. Somewhere between the Mafia and Michelangelo there is an Italian reality we can we be proud of."

I waited, hearing only heavy breathing. Finally he said, "Okay, Leda, have it your way. But you better be right, because I don't want to be defending myself against an angry mob. You can fuckin' believe that I'm going to get some nasty phone calls and letters. Not that I give a shit, since I'm used to them."

* * *

Undaunted, I named non-Italian Paul Hardy the art director. Many people were surprised, and I could imagine the talk: "No Italian art director for an Italian magazine? That's what Italians do best, right? Draw, design."

For me this was yet another bias to try to overcome. If all Italians had such a great sense of design, why all the tacky madonnas and fountains in Bronx backyards?

Paul Hardy, still the art director at *Chief Executive*, would provide the genius necessary to execute the concept—without any Italian heritage. I still recall the day I told him I would be leaving *Chief Executive* to start a magazine about Italy and Italian Americans.

"Paul, would you like to join me and be the art director?"

His eyes widened and actually glistened with imminent tears. "Oh my God, Leda! Ever since I was a kid growing up in Salt Lake City, I have wanted to be Italian." (He was a Mormon of English stock.) "I used to go to the movies to watch *Breaking Away* over and over. I identified with the main character who so wanted to be Italian. If I join you, will I get to go to Italy?"

"You bet," I fired back and embraced him. "This is too good to be true."

And it was, though Paul's talent and vision made *Attenzione* an award-winning magazine.

* * *

With this important aspect of the magazine secure in Paul's hands, I was free to move about the Italian American community and thoroughly enjoy the perks of my position.

Jeno came to New York regularly and conducted meetings in the living room of his suite at the Carlton House. We spent a lot of time talking about the cost of circulation and ways that we could locate and target Italian Americans with our subscription promotions. Many Italians had changed their names or, like Jeno, bastardized them.

Exactly what would go into the direct-mail packages describing the new magazine? It was my firm belief that *Attenzione* should appeal both to Italian Americans interested in their heritage and to Italophiles who loved Italy and everything about it.

I argued that the main message should be, "You don't have to be Italian to enjoy *Attenzione*, the magazine that celebrates the Italian lifestyle, past and present." With the help of Paul Goldberg, our circulation consultant, I convinced Jeno that the market for the magazine was much larger than just Americans of Italian heritage, although the primary thrust of our subscription efforts would be what magazine marketing specialists call an "ethnic select" list of names, identified for us as Italian.

Jeno never ate lunch at those meetings and often forgot to ask the rest of us if we were hungry. Finally, when our energy began to flag, we were allowed to order room service, but then only simple food that could be quickly and quietly consumed.

Many an evening I was driven to meetings to speak about the magazine and Italy to fraternal organizations such as the Sons of Italy or Unico. I was always surprised by how few in the audience had ever been to Italy. I saw an opportunity to encourage travel to the old country through editorial content and advertising. Thinking about this, I would doze in the back of the limousine while returning to Manhattan from neighboring Queens or New Jersey, where most of these organizations were based.

One day, Jeno declared that I should make a promotional visit to Italy to acquire advertising commitments and in some cases bypass the New York ad agencies. I didn't argue with him.

The idea of going to Italy as a V.I.P. and not a mere tourist was exciting beyond words. I would fly first class, Alitalia, stay in first-class hotels, have sit-downs with high-level government officials and businessmen. They would accept the request from legendary Jeno Paulucci to meet me; they would listen to my presentation and the reasons why they should support *Attenzione* magazine. Jeno's power paved the way for success. Moreover, that a woman was heading this ambitious project titillated Italian men. Jeno's reputation as a tough guy implied that I too was a person to be respected and reckoned with. My prior experience with unruly entrepreneurs had prepared me for the unexpected.

If Jeno's endorsement opened doors, the traditional Italian way of doing business guaranteed success. Influence peddling and one-hand-washes-the-other are basic Italian tenets that reach to the highest level. After all, this was where the Mafia originated. One favor—or slight— begets another.

Meetings were arranged for me with the kingpins of state-run companies, including Italcable (Italy's AT&T), the Italian state railroads, the tourism board of Sicily and other provinces, and Fiat in Turin. My bodyguard and guide was Jeno's cousin.

My fluent Italian was also key to my success since none of the men spoke English. Italians are notoriously unmotivated to learn English, and it was not uncommon to meet a chief executive or government official who could not speak a word of it.

What I tried to convey was the important role *Attenzione* would play in encouraging Italian Americans to travel to Italy and rediscover their roots, a great boost to tourism. Beyond that, the magazine would enhance Italy's image, which was still much in need of polishing. Our job was to combat the negative Hollywood stereotypes of Italian Americans.

It had occurred to me that Jeno himself fit the profile of a short, stocky Italian from the lower part of Italy or, as it is called, "the bottom of the boot." He walked aggressively and usually carried a large envelope-style briefcase under his arm, which somehow added to his swagger, bringing to mind James Cagney at his toughest. Despite this demeanor, I never feared him, even when overhearing his brutal conversations with underlings.

"Hey, Mark, what the hell! What's happening at the plant? I understand some guy in Jersey is refusing to distribute the last shipment of pizza because he says the pepperoni is rancid. Tell that motherfucker that I'll be there tomorrow, and I'll personally eat the fuckin' pizza and if I don't croak, he'll ship the stuff. Who the hell does he think he is? The Catholic Church?"

This was the same man who met with presidents and diplomats and chief executives, who was building political influence with Carter and Mondale (his Minnesota buddy). This was the same man who called me one day in January 1980 to say, "Hey, Leda, how would you like to go to dinner at the White House with me? They're having a state dinner for the president of Italy. We'll fly down in my plane."

When I caught my breath, I was about to ask why his wife wasn't accompanying him when he added, "Lois doesn't like these things." This prompted me to wonder how many of those "things" she'd been to.

As promised, we flew to DC on Jeno's Lear jet. I hand-carried aboard precious cargo: on a hanger and protected by a large garment bag, the beautiful red silk gown with matching floor-length evening coat I'd shopped so carefully for. That outfit is immortalized in the photo of me shaking hands with President Carter and President Cossiga.

Once again we stayed at the Hay Adams and that evening arrived at the White House in a long black limousine. I entered the lobby with

Jeno and climbed the grand stairway to the dining room, where my name was announced. I walked alone into the immense room, which is the custom.

Don't trip, I thought. *Stand up straight. Smile.*

I was ushered to a table glistening with candelabra and tall flower arrangements and set with china and silver as I had seen only in Tiffany. The room was filled with dignitaries, and all the movement—the waiters serving in their black formal outfits, the guests conversing with one another—seemed orchestrated in slow motion, like a stage play. Wine was poured in tall crystal glasses, and plates were removed and replaced with amazing grace. I ate little, afraid of having to talk with my mouth full.

I sat next to Umberto Nordio, the chairman of Alitalia, and I suddenly felt proud to be an American. We weren't oafs. We could be as classy as any European dynasty. Although I'd glimpsed similar events on television and in the movies, I'd never fully appreciated how regal the White House is.

Later, back at the hotel, Jeno, Nordio, and I sat in the cocktail lounge. I listened while they talked. Mostly they discussed the difference between the United States and Europe. At one point they lapsed into a comparison between Italian and American women. They reached quick agreement that Italian women were dedicated to pleasing a man and American women were teases. They talked and I gazed about the room, pretending not to hear. They seemed to forget I was there, or maybe they just didn't care. No matter—I knew my place and didn't take the bait. I was only a woman in a red dress.

* * *

In 1981, *Attenzione* was awarded the National Magazine Award for design, the American Society of Magazine Editors' most prestigious award in the industry.

When the announcement was made in the ballroom of the Waldorf Astoria, I stayed in my seat and pushed Paul Hardy out of his. "Go. You deserve it," I whispered. The buzz grew louder as Paul made his way to the podium: "Who is that guy?"

We tried to capitalize on the attention by taking out full-page ads in the *New York Times* bearing this headline, "The new American hero is a two-year-old with an accent."

The ad copy read: "The A.S.M.E. award for excellence in design went to *Attenzione*, which lives up to its name. Its design gains attention but less unto itself than to the content and spirit. The magazine's editor and art director have achieved a rapport that expresses itself in beautiful and always appropriate layouts. The approach to design is *con brio,* as the Italians say it."

We seemed headed in the right direction. We certainly were getting the right kind of recognition, and no one could say that *Attenzione* was just another weak attempt by zealous amateurs to produce an ethnic-pride magazine. *Attenzione* had broad appeal. The Missoni issue, which imaginatively used a photograph of the signature Missoni fabric on the cover, included pictures of the Missoni family in natural settings in Italy. This issue stands the test of time in terms of editorial quality and design. (And Paul Hardy realized his dream of going to Italy.)

But while we were receiving laudatory press from the professionals, in the background we heard simmering criticism from some who wanted a more strident voice raised against Italian stereotyping and prejudice and from others who had hoped to use the magazine for self-promotion. Every day we received press packages from Italian companies and businessmen telling us why they qualified for an article in the magazine, or in some cases the cover shot. If we had caved, *Attenzione* would have looked like a yearbook filled with bad photographs of swarthy Latin men sandwiched between articles about their companies.

Although we were dedicated to building Italian pride, we also did not shy away from issues involving the mob. But when our exposé of the Mafia-dominated garbage-hauling business appeared, we cut too close to the bone.

"Leda, what the hell do you think you're doing? You want to get me killed? Are you out of your fuckin' mind?"

Jeno was scared, and his call sent a clear message: retribution wasn't just something that happened in the movies. My naïveté was just that, and I would discover in the next six months that there were forces working on Jeno to bring us down.

In retrospect the exposé was foolish, and people were right to challenge my judgment. In our weekly editorial meetings, the wisdom of this article was discussed. In the end, I was asked to exercise more caution. "Lay off the exposés unless they are about Italy," I told the staff.

We did a profile on Sindona, the financier whose ties to the Vatican are alluded to in *The Godfather Part III*. This piece legitimized our ability to do investigative reporting without spotlighting gangsters and thus reinforcing the perception that Italian Americans were all beholden to the Mafia. The Sindona piece established us as a magazine capable of serious journalism.

I remain amazed at how recklessly I operated in a world that had a real underworld. Why did I think I was invincible? Where did I find the nerve?

* * *

One day I ran into Mort at le Cirque, New York's renowned restaurant. At first it was awkward because Le Cirque had been *our* place; we had spent many a romantic evening sitting at one of the pink banquettes. As I took my seat, my heart began to palpitate, and I smiled at him nervously. He was sitting with his friend Allen Boorstein, who became visibly nervous, as though fearing a scene.

When Mort got up to leave, he gave me a nod. Later that evening he called.

And that was it. With no review of the past, with no anger or recrimination, we began to date. Why would I go back to someone I had rejected so bitterly, with whom I had exchanged such hateful words? I knew it made no sense. I rationalized—romanticized—his jealous rages as love in the operatic sense. I had grown up on opera with its dramatic scenes of jealous lovers killing their beloved. Was that the ultimate expression of passionate love?

Part of me was flattered. Did he love me so much that he couldn't bear to lose me? No one else had fought so hard to have me. Certainly not Howard, whose dedication to calm reserve never permitted a vengeful act. Having someone battle for me, especially someone like Mort whom other women coveted, appealed to my competitive side.

But in the end, I returned to him because I missed him. Or I missed a man in my life, something I only reluctantly admit.

I didn't dare tell my mother, or anyone else for that matter, because I was ashamed, like a drug addict returning to a bad habit. Still, Mort's reentry into my life provided much needed comfort in that tumultuous year, 1981.

* * *

Even as *Attenzione* was being showered with accolades, Jeno was growing impatient. After three years, return on investment was disappointing, certainly not what he had become accustomed to in the packaged-food business. He was also hearing criticism from business associates making cheap jokes about the magazine. Most of his associates in Minnesota were not Italians, and they never ceased to rib Jeno about his Italian roots.

We were being recognized for our accomplishments, which should have given Jeno some sense of pride, but his business acumen was being challenged. In response, he sent Carl Hill, one of his top executives, to visit our offices frequently. At the time I believed that Hill was to monitor our activities, to assure Jeno that we were not wasting money. But in reality he was on a fact-finding mission in preparation for divesting themselves of the company.

Then, one day in the fall of 1981, Hill came into my office and closed the door. "Leda, I'm sorry to have to tell you this, but Jeno wants either to close the magazine or sell it."

"Carl, why?" My hands began to shake and my heart began to beat wildly. I felt dizzy and feared I would faint.

"Leda, we've invested several million dollars here, with no light at the end of the tunnel. Jeno's had it. Do you think you can find a buyer for it? If so, please work on that option. Alternatively, Jeno will lend you $250,000 to buy the company, but then you're on your own. We want to close the deal by January first, for tax purposes."

As soon as Carl left my office, I called Mort, still shaking. I explained what had happened and waited for his response. He was appropriately comforting.

"Don't worry, baby," he said confidently. "We'll figure this out. I knew this son-of-a-bitch's reputation was true. Meet me at Caminetto and we'll talk."

* * *

Between Thanksgiving and Christmas, I knocked on every door and called on every publishing company, trying to find a parent for the fledging publication. Over and over I heard the same thing: the audience for *Attenzione* is too narrow and the content too specialized to provide an appealing financial opportunity. "It's a special-interest magazine with too narrow a focus," was the mantra.

In its December issue, *Media Industry Newsletter* announced, incorrectly, that *Attenzione* magazine was being sold to its publisher, Leda Sanford. It also revealed that Jeno had offered to lend me $250,000 to get me started while I pursued other avenues of finance.

About then, my financially savvy stepfather Todd cautioned me. "Leda, a quarter of a million won't even give that magazine two more months of life. Then what? Believe me, you don't want to experience bankruptcy."

It was over. And to add a dash of bitterness and betrayal, the people who took over *Attenzione* reinforced the very stereotypes we had hoped to dispel.

In an angry phone call to Jeno, I vented recklessly. "How could you do this, Jeno? What about all your high-flown talk about giving back and doing something for your heritage? About fighting the negative image of Italians? How can you throw away this magnificent tribute to Italians?"

I had never spoken to anyone this way. Hysterical, I pressed on: "Have you any idea how much heart, talent, and emotion have gone into producing this magazine? No one will ever do it again, and you would have had the honor and pride of having created something better than a pizza!"

Jeno's response was swift. I left with no severance or any other tangible asset to show for three and a half years of passionate investment. All I had were some extremely complimentary letters from some top publishing executives. As I reread them, they sounded more like sympathy letters sent to someone who had just lost a loved one.

11. LIFELINE

With the loss of *Attenzione*, a profound feeling of failure enveloped me. My love for that magazine has never been equaled by any material thing or job.

Having Mort back in my life gave me hope and spurred my recovery. When we'd broken apart so publicly and with such rancor, reconciliation had seemed impossible. Now he was there for me.

Mort had always been fun. He had a great sense of humor and a way of making amusing comments about ordinary things that always made me laugh. Now we vowed that neither of us would stray, and he would limit the vodka to dinner. We returned to our usual restaurants, where people were well aware of our history. We attended industry functions, causing some heads to turn, but it didn't bother us.

A few friends had the temerity to ask what had drawn me back to Mort after what he'd done. There was no simple answer, but they accepted the fact that I loved him.

Now we chose to maintain our separate residences just a few blocks from each other. Typically, he would go home to change and pick up his clothes for the next day and then come to the Phoenix to spend the night. It was the ideal blend of intimacy and privacy.

Meeting him for dinner at one of our favorite restaurants always cheered me up after a discouraging and exhausting day of job hunting.

* * *

In the spring of 1982, I received a call from Jack Decker, vice president of Knapp Communications, which published *Architectural Digest, Bon Appétit, Geo,* and *Home Magazine.* I had met Jack when he was at N.W. Ayer, and I had called on him for advertising when I was with *Attenzione.*

"Leda, I'd like to talk to you about joining the Knapp organization. When are you available?"

"Any time you say, Jack," I said enthusiastically. Knapp was considered a premier publisher.

"Fine. How about tomorrow afternoon? We have just taken office space on Madison Avenue."

"I'm looking forward to it."

The Knapp organization, with its flagship *Architectural Digest,* had been based in Los Angeles, but they were relocating to New York. The next day I met Jack, and he described the vision Bud Knapp, the company founder, had for its growth.

"Leda, we have big plans for Knapp. We think we can be another Condé Nast.

"As you know, we recently acquired *Geo.* We have a fine editor for *Bon Appétit,* but we need to find some new revenue streams. We can't rely simply on food and wine advertisers. Look at *Food and Wine* magazine. If it wasn't associated with American Express it couldn't survive. We need new categories—some beauty pages, maybe even some automotive advertising."

After listening to the job description, smiling and nodding the whole time, I said, "Jack, I can't think of another magazine I'd rather represent. I know I can do this."

"Great, Leda. Bud Knapp is eager to meet you, so I'll set up an appointment."

Bud Knapp was an ebullient, overweight man with an engaging smile. I liked him and the interview went well. As we were winding down, he cleared his throat and said, "Now there is something I have to ask because I don't want any bad press. What's the status of your relationship with your ex-boyfriend?"

"Bud, that's all been resolved. In fact we are reconciled and plan to marry."

Mort had asked me to marry him after the demise of *Attenzione*, but given our tumultuous history, I hesitated. Now, with no work prospects and diminishing financial self-sufficiency, marriage seemed like a safe port in a storm. I had to admit it—I wanted someone to take care of me. Mort was now vice president in charge of licensing and merchandising for Playboy Enterprises.

As we were lying in bed after a romantic evening, Mort repopped the question: "Isn't it about time we made this legal?"

I kissed him and ran my fingers through his wavy hair. "Why not?" I said. "I think I'm ready."

In March of 1982, Mort and I married. The wedding was held at the Park Avenue Presbyterian Church on Park Avenue and Sixty-third Street, and the small, family dinner was held at the Sign of the Dove on Sixty-fifth and Third. My mother looked on approvingly, hoping I'd now be taken care of. My sons and Mort's two daughters, aged eleven and thirteen, were also there, wearing the same hopeful expressions. I was moderately happy. At least I was happy that I was making other people happy. And like most brides, I felt as if I had won something.

Six weeks later I became publisher of *Bon Appétit*.

* * *

Knapp Communications had been a one-publication, Los Angeles–based, privately owned entity driven by the success of *Architectural Digest*, conceived by Paige Rense, the editor-in-chief.

Like many regional home magazines, it had been an outlier. But Rense had been able to transcend those limitations by developing close relationships with the most influential interior decorators in New York. Like me, Rense had risen to the top without putting in a thirty-year stint at Condé Nast. She started out at the *Digest* in 1970, when that interior design quarterly was limping along with a circulation of 50,000. Twelve years later, she had boosted that number to 650,000.

In an effort to build a major publishing company, Knapp had acquired *Geo* from a German publisher, as well as *Home Magazine* and *Bon Appétit*, the latter an offshoot of yet another failed culinary magazine. He then opened sales and marketing offices in Manhattan.

In Los Angeles, I attended a celebratory dinner for the new management. Bud Knapp lurched to the podium and delivered a recklessly optimistic talk about our future. He was obviously drunk, and his speech was peppered with obscenities, which I found disturbing. Jack Decker was visibly embarrassed. He leaned over to me and said, "Please don't share this with anyone." Others just rolled their eyes, as though they'd seen it before.

I soon learned that *Geo* was plagued by financial problems; ad sales were dismal. *Home Magazine* was also struggling. And now the burden of generating cash flow for those ailing magazines would be borne by *Architectural Digest* and *Bon Appétit*.

I threw myself wholeheartedly into the challenge, and my list of accomplishments during my brief stint looks good on my résumé. I reversed the decline in ad lineage and increased total ad pages; I developed an advertising campaign around the theme of "the *Bon Appétit* life" and produced a booklet and audio-visual presentation entitled "The Food Enthusiast," which described the purchasing behavior of *Bon Appétit* subscribers and became a highly effective sales tool. All in less than a year.

I thought I was safe at last, in the bosom of a normal publishing company, doing business by the book.

I noticed that every day after lunch the doors of the publishers' offices were closed. As I soon found out, big lunches and two martinis required a nap.

In August 1982, *Adweek*, a trade journal, ran an article profiling the new women publishers. Coincidentally, the author was John Mack Carter, who wrote, "Leda Sanford's experience may be greater than that of any woman in the field." I was now in the company of such stars as Cathleen Black and Patricia Carbine, both highly regarded luminaries in publishing. Upon reflection, I think this spotlight trained on me exacerbated Paige Rense's irritation over the presence of another woman on the Knapp team.

Although I was exhilarated by the new challenge and enjoying my beautiful office on Madison Avenue, I couldn't ignore the discomfort I felt. And Paige Rense, long accustomed to being the queen bee, had given me the cold shoulder from day one. My invitations to Rense that we have lunch were never accepted.

The high point of my tenure at Knapp was orchestrating a promotional luncheon for advertisers at Cote Basque, the only time that exclusive restaurant was ever closed for a private luncheon. The event received much press, perhaps too much for Paige, who for a day was displaced from center stage.

One day Knapp president, Jack Decker, who had recommended me to Knapp, was discharged and replaced with Harry Myers as top dog. I was shocked by this abrupt—and seemingly unjustified—dismissal.

At the reception welcoming Harry as our new chief, I could feel that my handshake and words of congratulations were not warmly received. Harry's attitude had probably been forged by rumors—many of them exaggerated—of my colorful and unorthodox past. He never seemed to like me; he barely acknowledged me in the hallway.

He was an uptight man, a male chauvinist relic of the fifties, typical of publishers of that time. I was reminded of the man in the gray flannel suit with narrow lapels, leaving promptly at five to catch the New Haven Railroad to Westchester and his lily-white, suburban life. My pronouncements to the press about repositioning *American Home* to appeal to the "new woman" looking for fulfillment outside of the home must have infuriated him.

In meeting after meeting, Paige projected antagonism for nearly every idea I proposed. She had persuaded Bud to acquire *Bon Appétit* with the promise that she could reprise the miracle she had achieved at *Architectural Digest*. I believed the formula that had worked at *Architectural Digest* was not applicable here.

My affection for the editorial side of the business did me no good. I had been hired to increase sales, to develop a sales strategy, and to sell, sell, sell. Any attempt to influence the editorial department, still based in Los Angeles, was considered mutiny. As I saw it, Paige was trying to establish herself as editorial director for the entire company, and I was a threat since I had a track record of directing the development of a few magazines, including the award-winning *Attenzione*.

Despite the overt antagonism, I was totally unprepared for what happened when Harry Myers called me into his office one day. Constantine Kazanes, the human resources director, was there too. After we were all seated, Harry got right to it.

"You're fired," he said coldly.

Feeling as if I had been shot, I slumped in my chair and blurted out, "Why?"

"Because I don't like you and never have."

There was nothing more I could say. Even if I had found the words, I couldn't have uttered them. My mouth was dry, my throat tight.

Feeling as though I was going to have a heart attack, I stumbled out of the room and into my office. No sobbing—it was just too unbelievable. I called my stepfather, Todd, and told him I'd been terminated and to please call my mother. I was worried how she would take it.

Then I called Mort. The expletives flew from his mouth. "Goddamn bastards! What the fuck? Just leave the office right now. I'll meet you at home."

To sue or not to sue for wrongful termination—that was the biggest question we discussed. But lawyers pointed out that a lawsuit would bring the wrong kind of publicity, making it more difficult for me to find another job.

So I let it go.

The *New York Times* reported the event and best explained for me what had happened:

"Harry Myers, recently named group publisher at Knapp Communications, has brought in Robert S. Phelps, a former associate at the Meredith Corporation, to be the publisher of *Bon Appétit*. He replaces Leda Sanford, 49 years old, who has resigned. Mr. Phelps, 44, was advertising director of Meredith's *Metropolitan Home*, where Mr. Myers had been publisher."

My feelings for *Bon Appétit* and Knapp are best reflected in the fact that, although I have a collection of the various magazines I worked on, I do not have even one issue of *Bon Appétit* from that era.

12. JOSEPHINE

Rivulets of rain streamed down the large windows that embraced the corner of my bedroom. The view from nineteen stories above the city was normally breathtakingly beautiful; now it was just breathtaking. Windswept rain swirled about, lashing anything in its path with a fury only achieved when nothing stands in the way. The Phoenix, rising well above the surrounding buildings, seemed to take the brunt of the storm.

The howling wind, the drenching rain—they just reinforced my feelings of despair and defeat. One question haunted me: What was I going to do now?

Listless, I dressed for dinner. After wrapping myself in my Ralph Lauren ankle-length raincoat, I grabbed my umbrella and went to meet Mort at Il Caminetto. It was only two blocks away, which spared me the difficulty of trying to find a taxi in a Manhattan rainstorm.

I wished I knew how to drink, the way other people did. For many, it effectively dulled the senses and banished sadness and pain. The best I could do was a single Lillet on the rocks with a slice of orange. I had been culturally conditioned that drinking was to be avoided. My Italian family drank wine only with dinner and looked down on people who hung out at bars. At age nineteen, I'd married a Southerner who had also been raised to avoid liquor, as most Methodists in his area were, because it led to bad behavior.

Mort had a vodka and set about to cheer me up. "You should start your own consulting business," he said. "You've had so much experience in start-ups and new magazine development. And that's what you really like—inventing new magazines, right? You could work from home."

It was not an original idea—some friends had already suggested it—but it had appeal. It would allow me to limit travel, focus on my family, and maybe—just maybe—provide me with a more balanced life. We had Mort's children every other weekend, and maintaining the weekend house we'd acquired in Quogue on Long Island was increasingly my responsibility.

"Consultant"—I liked the sound of that. Mort and I spread the word, and soon—thanks to some recommendations from publishing friends—I had several clients. My first, a lawyer, wanted a business plan for a magazine entitled *Crime*. No problem, I could do that. The magazine editorial formula is a basic recipe that works for any subject.

I drafted the editorial plan for the magazine and created the recipe. Although skeptical at first, I came to believe a market might actually exist for this product. The publication was aimed at the crime buff in us all, piquing our curiosity about the dark side of human behavior. There had been some successful crime magazines in the thirties and forties, mostly detective magazines. But when I laid out the revenue requirements from advertising and magazine sales, the numbers shook the client's enthusiasm for the idea and he decided to lose his money some other way.

My most interesting project was *Living Anew*, a magazine for people living on their own. It was a timely idea, but as usual, the entrepreneur who thought of it had no concept of how much time and money it takes to build a subscription base. Readers, of course, are what advertisers are buying. Once again, when the idea people confronted the cost of building a loyal readership, their enthusiasm faded.

* * *

In the spring of 1985, Mort, my mother, my stepfather, and I decided to go to Europe. My mother, Josephine, had remarried ten years earlier at age sixty-five to a successful CEO, Todd Cole, president of CIT Financial (he was fifty-five). She had been enjoying the best years of her life.

Mort and I flew to Paris and then drove leisurely through the magical chateau country in France to the Riviera and on to Montecatini in Tuscany. My mother and Todd met us there with a few other friends.

While we were all together, Mom began to complain of severe stomach pains. Upon returning to New York, she was diagnosed with terminal cancer.

I put aside my consulting work from July 1985 until December, when she passed away. Till then I spent every day with her. We revisited memories, good and bad, and laughed and cried. We thumbed through the photo albums she had kept so meticulously. They took us back to Italy, the Bronx, the Catskill Mountains, where my sister and I spent summers on a friend's farm with my grandmother. The photographs captured the intricate fabric of lives lived on two continents in two cultures. There was my first communion; my graduation from Christopher Columbus High School; Grandpa walking me down the aisle to marry Howard; my sister wearing a swimsuit with a banner that said, "Miss New Rochelle."

Mom lived in a fashionable apartment on Fifth Avenue and Eighty-ninth Street. Each day I would walk rapidly to and from Sixty-fifth street to Eighty-ninth in my jogging suit and sneakers. At night I would curl up on the burgundy velour sofa in my living room. I dreaded going to bed because I couldn't sleep. Mort would leave the room with the same emotionless words every night. "I'm packing it in. Good night." No kiss on the forehead, no pat on the shoulder. Only Atavin got me through it.

Although Mort could be supportive, this situation was more than he could handle. And perhaps my sad preoccupation with my mother caused him to find solace in the attention of other women, continuing a lifelong pattern of using women to escape from life's harsher realities. Mort's mother had died when he was eleven, leaving him with a father who was not warm or attentive. Women had become his surrogate mothers. Now there were a few women in his office and other old flames who appeared on the scene now and then. That raised my suspicions, but not enough to distract me from the more serious situation.

Around Thanksgiving, my mother was readmitted to St. Vincent's Hospital, intensive care. She had private nurses round the clock and, heavily medicated, was in no pain.

When the doctor informed us that she had only a couple of weeks left, I knew I didn't want her to die alone in the hospital.

"It's my mother's wish—and mine too—that she be released and come home," I told the doctor.

He was unmoved. "I'm sorry, but she should stay here." He gave no explanation.

I was told she couldn't leave without the doctor's signature on a formal release. I could not accept this and had never been one to bend to authority. I asked Todd to have the car outside the front entrance the next morning. We agreed on the time. At the hospital, I told the private nurse to get a wheelchair, which she reluctantly did.

Working quickly, quietly, the nurse and I put Mom in the wheelchair and wrapped her in a blanket. With my heart pounding, I opened her door a crack and scanned the hallway for anyone who might want to stop us. With the coast clear, we scurried down the hall to the elevator. Once on the first floor, we bypassed the reception area and zoomed out to the waiting car. Todd was at the wheel with the motor running. We got Mom in, slammed the doors, and the car pulled away. My palms were sweating, my body trembling.

Once we arrived home and got Mom into her bed, she actually smiled. She was glad to be back home. Todd and I hugged each other in relief. That night I slept peacefully, knowing that I had rescued her, just as she had rescued me so many times.

I sat with her in her bedroom every day for the next couple of weeks. One day, near the end, she suddenly announced that she could see her mother. "She's smiling," she said.

On her last day, they increased the morphine. With Todd nearby, I held her in my arms. Her last word was simply "Leda."

I didn't cry. I didn't hide in my room. There were people who needed me to be strong, including my sons, for whom I always tried to be an example of strength and dignity. Todd was devastated and needed comforting. And my sister, who arrived too late to say good-bye, was angry with me because she felt I had not made it clear how close to death our mother was.

As for me, I'd lost my safety net. More and more I realized my mother had given me the courage to take chances. Her loving enthusiasm for everything I did was the impetus for my personal drive to excel. She had always made me feel special, smart, and capable. She relished my success. Among her belongings, I found neatly kept files with news clippings heralding my every professional accomplishment. She felt proud—and vindicated.

My mother's death plunged me into relentless remembering. With a new perspective forged by her death, I admired her courage anew. Her greatest act of defiance had been leaving my father after spending a year with him in Italy. I was fifteen that November of 1949 when we boarded the SS *Italia* in Genoa and set sail for New York, already my fifth trip across the Atlantic.

She left him—with great difficulty, she claimed—because she felt my potential could not be fulfilled in a country where a woman's place was in the home. My father, though educated himself, did not believe in higher education for women.

My sister Paola took a different path. Partly because she had been a frail child and didn't like school, my mom assumed she would follow the traditional route to marriage and family life. In Paola's own way, she defied traditional expectations. She married, divorced, married again in her early twenties, and became an internationally acclaimed yacht designer with a brilliant career.

As I sorted through Mom's belongings, memories came and went. Paintings my father had acquired and restored for sale put me back in his little Bronx art gallery watching him work. I could still smell the odor of the oil paint and linseed oil.

If Fausto had prevailed and we'd stayed in Italy, my life would have been different. Better? Worse? Hard to say, but I certainly wouldn't have become the independent feminist I ultimately became—uncompromising, combative, argumentative, and fearless in the face of difficulties and setbacks.

In Mom's final gesture of support, she left her entire financial estate to me. Although not a fortune, it provided a cushion for me and my kids, especially welcome since I was again out of work. She had always worried about my future. Plus, she doubted Mort's reliability and believed my sister, successful and solidly married, did not need help. Did she love me more than she loved Paola? She certainly had higher aspirations for me.

My mother's will created a schism between my sister and me. She didn't say anything at the reading of the will or for a while after. But in time she did unleash her feelings and spewed them out with venom. "I'm supposed to believe that she decided to do this on her own, that you didn't convince her to change her will?"

"Paola, is that what you think of me? I can't believe it. You know I'm not a liar or a cheat. This was entirely Mom's idea, with Todd's approval. How dare you accuse me of such a terrible thing?"

For the next twenty years, until my sister passed away in 2007, that tension remained between us.

* * *

In the summer of 1986, I took Scott, who had graduated from Syracuse University, to Europe without Mort. It was his graduation present, and I knew it would be the last time he would want to travel with his mother. We skipped Italy because of terrorist threats by the Red Brigade. Instead, we went to Switzerland, stopping in St. Moritz. Scott had the thrill of his life speeding on the winding roads through the Swiss Alps to Austria.

In Salzburg, we stayed with my close friend, Gheri Sackler, at her chalet. There we attended the enchanting Salzburg Music Festival. This is where *The Sound of Music* was filmed, and I found the idyllic beauty of those mountains even more healing than that joyful movie. It wiped away sadness and pain and rekindled my appetite for life.

13. "The Most Beautiful Magazine in the World"

"Thanks, Mom. That was a great trip," Scott said as our plane began to descend toward the Manhattan skyline. It had been a wonderful and unforgettable exploration of a part of Europe unfamiliar to most Americans. Spending two weeks alone with Scott, sharing discoveries and feelings more openly than we ever had at home, allowed us to bond, a closeness that has endured. We still reminisce about that trip: the chubby yodeler singing in a Swiss restaurant; the plush Hotel Dolder Grand, where an intimidating waiter railroaded Scott into ordering something he really didn't want.

On our return, Mort met us at the gate. "How vas the faderland?" he quipped, unable to resist his need to joke about everything.

"Oh Mort, for God's sake," I shot back, shaking my head disapprovingly. "That's not funny."

I had grown tired of his shtick before we left on the trip, but still immersed in the charm and sophistication of Europe, I now found it even more irritating than I remembered.

As we drove home, Scott did most of the talking, rattling on about the highlights of our trip. Mort rolled down his window and lit a cigar.

Home at last, I was not in the mood for any sexual celebration. I was too busy evaluating my past and future—worries about my career—to muster any desire. What's more, my growing distrust of Mort was interfering with my attraction to him. Several friends and colleagues had spotted Mort with other women. Whenever I confronted him, his excuse was always the same. "It was a business meeting, for heaven's sake."

But I knew he needed constant reaffirmation that other women found him attractive. He didn't always have to go to bed with them, but he needed to flirt. While such behavior seemed to boost his ego, it devastated mine. I couldn't control him and he was taking advantage of that. I didn't like losing, and that made me susceptible to attention from others.

In the morning, Mort and I talked over breakfast, first about the trip, then about the future. Should I go back to consulting or explore the job market?

We batted it back and forth, but it was all talk. Then I got the boost I needed—a call from Franco Maria Ricci, the internationally renowned publisher of highly prized art books and *FMR*, subtitled "the most beautiful magazine in the world."

"*Buon giorno*, Leda," he said. Switching to English with a heavy Italian accent, he introduced himself. "I am Franco Maria Ricci, and your name was given to me by several Italian businessmen here in New York. I understand you were responsible for developing *Attenzione?*"

"Yes, Signor Ricci, I'm very proud of that."

"Leda, I'm sure you are familiar with *FMR* and our activities here in the United States. We introduced the English version here a few years ago and were received with great enthusiasm. I'd like to meet with you and explain our situation and see if you would be interested in working with us. Can we meet this week?"

"Any time you say, Signor Ricci."

We set a time and he gave me the address of his office. It was a block from the Phoenix.

In preparation for that meeting, I did some homework. With no Internet at my disposal in 1986, I called a few key people who were familiar with the Italian business community. They were quick to fill me in. Ricci was revered in Italy for his publishing accomplishments. Not only did he produce the elegant magazine that bore his name, but he had been selected by major corporations in Italy to produce publications glorifying the various companies' histories.

Born a marquis in Parma, Italy, the birthplace of Gianbattista Bodoni, the creator of Bodoni font, Ricci was a preeminent printer who used only Bodoni. In 1970, he embarked on a monumental ten-year project: reprinting the *Encyclopédie de Diderot et Alembert*, a 10,500-page limited edition (three thousand copies), for which he received the Chevalier des Arts et des Lettres award from the French Republic.

The American edition—*FMR, The Magazine of Franco Maria Ricci*—had been launched with great fanfare in 1984. It was promoted as "the most talked-about magazine in Europe," where Ricci also produced Italian, French, and German versions. Printed on exquisite paper and perfect bound with a heavy, laminated glossy-black cover, it was the perfect coffee-table magazine.

Each issue contained four or five articles written by scholars or renowned authors such as Gore Vidal, Italo Calvino, and Noam Chomsky. The vivid full-page images, which included stunning frescos, palaces, and gardens, were suitable for framing.

FMR had initially attracted eighty thousand subscribers in the United States and some high-end advertisers, such as Bulgari, Alitalia, Fendi, and Ferrari. Despite the hype and generous press coverage, the company had stalled, and Ricci was searching for a solution.

He thinks I could be that solution, I thought.

With this meager background, I dressed my best and went to meet him. I felt confident. Besides years of experience in the magazine business, I was Italian born and fluent in the language. I had been here before … I could do this.

I was surprised at the modest offices of the fabled *FMR*. Nothing more than a three-room apartment on Sixty-fifth Street. The young woman who opened the door introduced me to Ricci, who, like so many upper-class Italian men, was rather short and effete. Dressed in a dark, well-tailored sport coat and open-collared white shirt, he had an impish quality I liked. He wore a red ceramic flower lapel pin, his trademark, as I'd learned in my research. Modestly handsome with piercing eyes, he took my outstretched hand and brushed it with a slight kiss.

As Ricci described his ambitious venture, I thought, *this is déjà vu.* He expressed his disappointment with the high cost of locating subscribers, which he called "members." As always, circulation loomed as the challenge. I sensed that the cost and effort necessary to reach the target audience and expand the reader base was daunting to Ricci. So far he had targeted only the elite. For an annual membership fee of forty-eight dollars, you received six issues of *FMR* and a membership card, good for discounts in his bookstores, as well as a handsome silk-bound address book.

Franco boasted about the elaborate black-tie launch party they had held at the New York Library and the glitterati in attendance. He shared press clippings full of accolades the magazine had received for its excellence. It had once been the talk of the town, challenging the supremacy of every upscale magazine from the *Robb Report* to *Architectural Digest*.

Now, after three years and without someone in New York to keep the momentum going, enthusiasm for this strange magazine was lagging. Apparently, the status that came with being able to afford it had lost its appeal.

After barely glancing at my résumé, Franco looked me in the eye and said, "I need a manager who will oversee every aspect of the American operation except editorial production. That's done in Italy. The magazine is sent to the States by container ship and then warehoused in Long Island City for distribution. I need a head of operations, someone to sell advertising, supervise subscriptions, and direct our publicity efforts."

He paused; I nodded, but before I could speak, he continued. "Soon I want to open a boutique in New York like the one we have in London. It will sell our entire product line—books, magazines, diaries. How do you feel about this, Leda?"

"Mr. Ricci—," I began

"No, no, no, you must call me Franco." Such familiarity surprised me, coming as it did from a marquis and supposedly the first person in his family to work in five hundred years.

Inside I was bubbling with excitement, but I maintained a formal tone when I said, "Franco, I am honored that you would entrust me with this unique project. I assure you, I have the experience required, and it will give me great personal satisfaction to contribute to your success."

Franco beamed. Emboldened, I asked for $6,000 a month in salary and a travel and entertainment budget. Franco readily agreed and we shook on it.

I could hardly wait to share the news with Mort and my kids. My new job relieved me of the insecurity of financial dependence on Mort. I called him first.

"Well, you did it again," Mort replied. "What's your secret? Those flashing Italian eyes?"

"Mort," I said with a lingering emphasis on his name, "maybe so. Is that why *you* hired me at *Men's Wear*?"

* * *

In contrast to my former positions, where I dealt daily with a manager, at *FMR* I reported directly to Franco. He soon left for Italy, telling me we would communicate by phone and fax. Meanwhile, I had to get up to speed quickly and identify the priorities needing my immediate attention. What was the number-one problem? Perception by the advertising community? Subscription renewal rate? The fact that subscription marketing was headquartered in the hinterlands of Lansing, Michigan?

Over the three and a half years I worked for *FMR*, I enjoyed the status of my association with Franco Maria Ricci. I also enjoyed not having to call on ad agencies. Instead, I dealt with CEOs and company presidents, men who with one phone call could dictate advertising commitments. I persuaded many a CEO to order gift subscriptions for their preferred clients.

Museums too loved the magazine, and my position opened doors to highly exclusive museum openings and parties reserved for major contributors. I was also welcomed extravagantly at the best Italian restaurants in New York.

Despite the glamour of this period, I knew *FMR* could not survive for long; it just didn't work financially. Certain I was getting out, I helped Franco locate a shop for his boutique as a final gesture of goodwill.

I began to explore the job market, even met with a few headhunters. I still shudder when I relive my meeting with one, who looked at my résumé, then at me, and coldly said, "Leda, you're too old. You're fifty-five. They're looking for thirty-five or younger. I suggest you get out of this business."

This was a crushing blow. Stoop-shouldered, I walked out of his office and down Lexington Avenue, stopping at store windows, seeing only the reflection of an old woman.

Was it possible, after working so hard to become proficient in my field, that I could simply be discarded? Too old? No, I had plenty of good years left.

Having recently read *Age Wave* by Ken Dychtwald, I had already become interested in the phenomenon of aging. The author's forecasts regarding aging baby boomers, especially the societal impact of their impending retirement, was intriguing. Now his book seemed especially relevant.

I began to see aging as my new cause. Coincidentally, I heard that *Modern Maturity*, the magazine of the American Association of Retired Persons, needed an advertising director. I found the name of the firm conducting the search for AARP, and defying conventional wisdom that high-end headhunters cannot be contacted directly by job hunters, I did just that—and got a meeting.

I went into that meeting with great confidence. I was, after all, highly qualified, with experience in advertising, circulation, and sales. But what AARP most needed was my ability to sell ideas, to change people's minds. Now I just had to sell myself.

I did well enough to make the first cut. Then I got a telephone call: the competition had narrowed to two candidates—me and an unnamed man.

We were flown separately to Washington DC to meet Horace Deets, the executive director, who would make the final decision. The interview covered the usual business issues, but it was my genuine passion for AARP's mission that connected with Deets.

"Mr. Deets, I am a mission-oriented person. The work I did at *American Home* was inspired by my interest in the women's movement, and *Attenzione* was another cause I could embrace. AARP's original mission—to change the image of aging—is a concept I can enthusiastically promote. I relish the opportunity to convince advertisers that the mature audience is worth talking to."

Months later, Deets revealed that what really impressed him was that I had read *Age Wave* and was so enthusiastic about changing people's attitudes about aging.

When the press announced that I was the new advertising director of *Modern Maturity* and the *AARP Bulletin*, most of the buzz focused on my professional agility. People wondered how I'd snatched this prize from so many capable *male* candidates. Although AARP was founded by a woman, top management had always been male.

Franco Maria Ricci was not bereft about my leaving, because *FMR* was struggling and Franco was growing weary and bitter. He blamed *FMR*'s declining success on the boorishness of Americans, a classic excuse of elitists.

* * *

As this chapter of my professional life was winding down, my relationship with Mort was deteriorating. The final straw was when I saw Chester Gore, president of his own ad agency, at the 21 Club before a luncheon.

"Leda, great to see you," he said gleefully. "I coincidentally was just talking to Mary Ann Sommers. She was all excited because she'd received a dozen red roses from Mort Gordon."

I felt my heart stop, then sputter forward. A full-body pain threatened to paralyze me. Doing my best to look unruffled, I could only respond, "Oh, really?" Somehow I got through that business luncheon without betraying how distressed I was—or so I imagined.

Sommers was a small-time player in the magazine business, who had created *Child* magazine with a partner and then sold it to the *New York Times*. I'd heard from colleagues that she was jealous of what I had achieved. Was this her way of one-upping me? That's the way it seemed. With my diminishing affection for Mort, I also wondered, *Why the hell do I care?*

That evening when Mort called me (he was in Paris on business), I confronted him. "I saw Chester Gore at 21, and he happened to mention that you sent roses to Mary Ann Sommers. You do like to send roses, don't you?" I spat.

Mort sensed my anger and responded in kind. "That's not true. He's lying! You know what a *yenta* he is."

"I don't believe you! I can never believe you! Why are you even with me?"

Refusing to give an inch, Mort lashed back. "I've heard of frequent sightings of you with Peter Faucetta."

I had in fact become close to Peter, a business associate I'd met while at *Attenzione*. He had been a comfort and an ego booster during the travail of my personal and professional life. He was handsome, he was debonair, and our friendship was to endure for more than twenty years.

"I do business with him," I shot back. "You know that."

I couldn't admit the truth: I was having an affair with Peter. So why was I so upset by Mort's infidelity if I too was being unfaithful? Maybe because he had done it first and more often. In any event, we were obviously heading down the same path again—a rocky ride of mistrust and recriminations.

Before our life degenerated into another acrimonious melodrama, we agreed to divorce. Fortunately, we had kept our separate apartments.

14. MODERN MATURITY

Divorce is never an enjoyable experience, even when you desperately want out of a marriage. It brings out the worst in the best of people. It's even worse when you detest failure.

To minimize the ugliness, I didn't fight for anything tangible, neither for alimony nor for the house in Quogue. That was no small sacrifice, as my sons and I loved that summer place. Scott and I had found it while house hunting together one spring; I had enjoyed decorating it and retreating to it with or without Mort and the kids. As a family we'd had some great times there.

What's more, owning a house in the Hamptons was a highly visible status symbol for successful New Yorkers. Giving up that lifestyle and giving up on my relationship with Mort, something I had grappled with for almost twenty years—it all made me feel sick. Lying in bed at night, I sometimes felt a searing sense of loss, as if I'd severed a limb. But this was no phantom pain—it was real. It reminded me of the words more than one widow had used in my presence: "It's as if part of me has been amputated."

I hated giving up. Was that it?—I was giving up. Whatever you called it, the choice was between leaving Mort or sacrificing myself to someone I no longer liked or trusted. It was no choice.

I had put my family second when I began my journey of self-discovery and always carried a sense of guilt about it. But this was different. I couldn't live any longer with daily doubt about Mort's fidelity and veracity, robbed of the peace and security that allows one to function productively. Whether I wanted to believe it or not, I was getting older and needed to make the most of my remaining years—financially, emotionally, and experientially.

The new and challenging job I'd taken with AARP would be my salvation.

* * *

The offices of AARP's advertising department were located at 420 Lexington Avenue, a building that connected to Grand Central Station, one of my favorite spaces in New York.

On the appointed Monday morning, I arrived there punctually, pushed through the double-glass entry, and introduced myself to the receptionist. Bob Wood, the publisher, came out to meet me.

"Welcome, Leda, I see you found your way. Let me take you to your office, and then we've scheduled a meeting in the conference room so you can meet the staff."

We walked down a long corridor, past several windowless staff offices whose gloominess made me shudder. My office, in contrast, was spacious, strategically positioned in the corner with windows on two sides. Unfortunately, situated on the lowly fourth floor in one of Manhattan's midtown canyons, the windows offered no view and little daylight. Fluorescent lighting permeated the premises, producing a tiring effect for which there is no antidote except a walk in the country. Fortunately I would be out much of the time, calling on ad agencies, lunching with clients at the best restaurants, and traveling to see potential advertisers all over the country, just as I'd done before.

The staff people, trapped at their desks from nine to five, had no respite. Years later I often scan the masthead of the magazine looking for familiar names. Some are still there, with slightly elevated titles, and I ponder their lives spent incarcerated in that dismal building, living for retirement benefits.

The headquarters of ARRP were in Washington, the main advertising department in Manhattan, and the editorial department in Long Beach, California. There were sales reps in Chicago, Detroit, Dallas, Atlanta, Los Angeles, and San Francisco. Travel to all those cities would be required, I was told, including trips to Long Beach every two months to sign off on the final layout.

The magazine's ad income was projected to be $50 million for the upcoming year. The cost of a full-page ad, which would reach twenty-two million members, was $220,000. Only a few companies were willing to write that check, especially if they were only reaching people over fifty. I often joked that only generals could afford to advertise in *Modern Maturity*: General Motors, General Foods, and General Electric.

At least I had no worries about circulation revenue—the magazine was an AARP member benefit. Annual dues were twelve dollars, half of which funded the magazine. It was a relief not to have to worry about replacing subscribers or enticing them into subscribing in the first place. We didn't even have to monitor newsstand sales.

My title was advertising director of the Maturity Magazines Group. I was responsible for ad sales for the bimonthly *Modern Maturity* magazine and the monthly *AARP Bulletin* newspaper, each with a circulation of twenty-two million and combined gross revenues of $70 million.

The transition from working with "class" magazines like *Attenzione, Bon Appétit*, and *FMR* to the ultimate "mass" magazine would be a stretch. The former targeted the deep-pocket elite; AARP targeted the hoi polloi.

My primary responsibility was setting sales and marketing strategies and providing direction and support for both the sales staff in the New York office and independent reps around the country. It was a big job, but I had plenty of help. In fact, I'd never before had such human and financial resources at my command.

Moreover, I came aboard just as top management had resolved to get serious about building ad revenue. "We want to operate more as a business than a nonprofit," I was told. Until then, they'd paid little attention to profitability, made no real effort to capitalize on the enormous reach their membership gave them. With more than twenty million readers, we could be the biggest player in the print medium for those wanting to reach the fifty-plus market

Much of my time was spent reorganizing the New York office. Making it more of a traditional publishing operation would allow us to compete aggressively for advertising from the big guys.

* * *

AARP had come a long way since it was founded by Ethel Percy Andrus in 1958. Andrus, a retired schoolteacher, had first started the National Association of Retired Schoolteachers, as well as the first-ever health insurance program for people over fifty. The National Association of Retired Schoolteachers eventually evolved into AARP. I had long been inspired by Andrus's writings on women and aging. She recognized how unprotected and vulnerable women are as they age, much more so than men.

Andrus believed that people didn't age; they atrophied. As they did less and less, retreating ever more from new challenges and experiences, they wasted away in every way—physically, mentally, and spiritually.

While working at AARP, it occurred to me that the organization itself had atrophied. AARP no longer made any effort to promote its founder's writings (though in 2008, on AARP's fiftieth anniversary, the editor of *Modern Maturity* did dedicate his editorial to her). As I discovered, few employees at *Modern Maturity* knew much about the original idealistic mission of the organization that paid their salaries. Most employees knew only that it 1) was a nonprofit and nonpartisan membership organization for people over fifty, 2) provided a wide range of benefits and products for its members, and 3) is one of the most powerful lobbying groups in the United States.

Making waves once again, I opined that *Modern Maturity* should be more vocal on women's issues, and that included our editorial content. Furthermore, our advertising should focus more on women's health problems rather than just targeting generic products for both sexes.

The biggest obstacle was the ad-standards department, a tyrannical arm of AARP, which evaluated all advertising materials and freely banished any products or services that projected a negative view of aging, in their opinion. Thus you saw no ads for funeral services, wheelchairs, or pharmaceuticals; and no ads that competed with AARP products, such as automobile insurance.

Particularly galling was the prohibition against ads for incontinence products, such as Depends and Serenity, which benefit both men and women. Two deep-pocket companies, Kimberly Clark and Johnson & Johnson, were competing for this market, but no matter how they tried to rework their ads, no matter how much they avoided mentioning the condition their products were supposed to remedy, they never made it past the ad-standards guardian.

I felt this policy was unreasonable and that it ignored the needs of our members, many of whom needed adult diapers. In an effort to find a compromise, I called on account managers from both Kimberly Clark and Johnson & Johnson.

My first visit was to the product manager for Serenity. Before I could roll out my ideas about how we might get around AARP's in-house censor, the bright-eyed manager abruptly produced a large adult diaper from behind his desk, stood, and said, "Watch this." Holding the open diaper in his left hand, he picked up a glass of water from his desk and poured its contents into the diaper. I instinctively shrank back, fearing imminent disaster. The diaper absorbed every drop.

"See! Eight ounces. Totally absorbed." He beamed as though he'd just discovered a loophole in the law of gravity. Temporarily and uncharacteristically speechless, I finally mustered, "Wow, that's impressive. But it doesn't solve the problem. Perhaps there's a way of showing the product's effectiveness that's a little more . . . subtle."

But apparently there wasn't. We never succeeded in overcoming AARP's objection to the product.

My enthusiasm for promoting a positive image of aging was inspired in part by the knowledge that a majority of the over-sixty population had quality-of-life health issues. Many also faced financial problems, forcing them to focus on AARP's discounts and member benefits. Developing innovative marketing programs that conformed to AARP's stringent standards was a constant battle for the entire sales staff.

I was constantly having to say something like this to one staff member or another: "Charlie, I know Bristol Meyers is a big advertiser, and I know how hard you've worked on this account, but if the agency won't make the text changes the ad-standards director has asked for, we can't accept the ad. Do you want me to join you on that call?"

"Well," Charlie said, "We can take those guys to lunch and schmooze them, Leda, but frankly I don't think they're going to change their copy just to please us. Let's face it, they don't need *Modern Maturity*. For about the same cost they can use television."

* * *

The annual sales meeting that year was scheduled for October in Beaver Creek, Colorado, a perfect time to connect with the sales and marketing people. As with most sales meetings, the stated goal was to get everyone charged up for maximum performance in the year ahead. I did none of the planning; my only responsibility was to bond with the team and present my sales strategy and new marketing ideas. This junket rivaled my trip to Ireland, minus the corporate jet. The craggy mountain scenery on the drive from Denver to Beaver Creek compared favorably with the sweeping landscapes I'd seen in Switzerland. The job certainly had its perks.

My sprawling suite in the luxurious Hyatt Regency seemed excessive for a nonprofit organization. The twenty-five-foot-long living room, the elegant dining room, the king-size beds, all decorated in a homey colonial style—it stunned me, and I had seen opulence before.

"Do I have the honeymoon suite?" I asked Ina Josephson, the staff person who had made the arrangements.

"No, Leda, it's the executive suite. We like to gather before dinner in the ad director's suite for cocktails. We find it breaks the ice and sets the right tone for the meeting."

Who was I to challenge tradition? As I saw it, that little cocktail party was a test of my mettle as an executive in the big leagues, and I passed. In the photographs documenting the event, my smiling face projects success.

* * *

Traveling allowed me to connect with Peter frequently. Before the days of e-mail, we would talk on the phone, coordinate our itineraries, and arrange to meet. I justified it because male executives had been doing it forever. Besides, that intimate relationship provided much-needed relief from the Byzantine world of AARP, brightening my heavy work load.

Although we met often, our clandestine reunions always electrified me. In another city, far from our native Manhattan where everyone knew us, we could be more expressive in public, although that was not truly in Peter's nature. Mostly, it was an opportunity for unbridled sex in an anonymous hotel room.

For now, that was enough for me. My life finally seemed on track; I was grateful and relatively happy. Marriage did not interest me. Freedom did.

Meanwhile, my son Robert, thirty-nine, had a job at E.A.T., the deluxe Upper East Side gourmet emporium. After years working in various capacities in restaurants around Manhattan, he had settled into a management position at this lively spot, allowing him to combine his love of food and people.

He was living with his young girlfriend—adventurous, cute, and a chef—while indulging his passion for law enforcement, mostly listening to police radio calls and volunteering for the police force.

Scott, five years younger, was still living at home and working as an account executive at Chiat-Day, one of New York's hottest ad agencies.

* * *

As the months wore on, I became increasingly intolerant of the sterile corporate environment of AARP. I suffered through long, deadly meetings in *Titanic*-sized conference rooms, meetings so mind numbing as to stifle any innovative idea that challenged the status quo. Despite this, I managed to develop marketing materials that were both novel and imaginatively presented. I took dry facts about the aging of America and dramatized them, driving home the message that advertisers needed to reach those consumers. For the first time, I enjoyed a budget sufficient to get the job done.

But I lacked the right people. I was supposed to be energizing my staff, spurring them on to new levels of achievement, but actually I wanted to replace them all. I think they could sense it.

My inability to hide my impatience did not help my standing at AARP. My face—mostly my eyes, I was told—often betrayed my feelings, no matter how neutral an expression I tried to adopt.

When I suggested we invite Ken Dychtwald, author of *Age Wave*, as keynote speaker at the annual convention, I blindly stepped on a landmine. He was considered too commercial, I was informed. When I pressed for clarification, I was made to feel like a heathen among the converted.

"We do not want to be a vehicle for capitalizing on this demographic shift," one executive exclaimed.

"Dychtwald is too focused on the commercial opportunities that lie in the aging of America," said another.

That made no sense to me, but I was done talking. I scanned the room for a window, some way to let light and air into the room. No windows, just a door; an exit from this place that I had so enthusiastically embraced a few months before. I finally had the money and the tools with which to accomplish great things, but I could feel the dream slipping away.

As advertising director I was supposed to refrain from editorial opinions. The wall was high between editorial and advertising. Controlling my desire to voice my opinion on the insipid or irrelevant content of *Modern Maturity* took extraordinary restraint. Although I had an excellent relationship with the editor, Henry Fenwick, he was justifiably concerned about jeopardizing his job and wasn't about to challenge the establishment. Top editorial jobs, particularly for middle-aged men, were at a premium.

I was most disturbed by the publication's avoidance of women's issues. Content focused primarily on uncontroversial subjects like nature, travel, and food preparation. The magazine went out of its way to avoid profiling mature celebrities like Clint Eastwood or Sophia Loren, lest AARP be criticized for setting unrealistic aging goals.

My suggestion that we segment the content, creating separate sections for men and women, was met with steely glances.

"The concept of a general-interest magazine went out with *Life* magazine," I said excitedly at one of our joint-planning meetings. "What is *Modern Maturity* anyway? A bimonthly can't be a news magazine. Is it a health magazine? Then we have to be sensitive to the unique health concerns of men and women. A clearer definition of the magazine would help our salespeople. What's more, we could provide page positions compatible with the products. Advertisers want to place ads adjacent to editorial that is supportive of what they're selling."

"AARP does not intend to prostitute itself in order to increase advertising," Henry Fenwick chimed in. "Our content has to have general appeal."

"Henry, there is a difference between general or mass appeal and watered-down content that doesn't really connect with anyone," I responded.

Now I had really stepped over the line. I saw it in their faces.

Chuck, who was chairing the meeting, brought the conflict to a halt with a condescending, "Well, that was an interesting exchange, guys. Now let's move on to our page forecast for the next issue."

"Guys"—that was a common way of addressing everyone, including women. It really bugged me, now more than ever. In fact, almost everything about this organization and its people bugged me.

15. California Dreamin'

I mustered my courage and walked into Publishing Director Chuck Allen's office. I carried promotional materials for Ken Dychtwald's first Age Wave conference, to be held in San Francisco in August 1992. Considering the antipathy that AARP had for him, I was more than a little apprehensive.

I began my pitch even before I sat down.

"I know AARP is not a fan of Age Wave, but I just received this invitation. It's going to be a ground-breaking conference." I handed Chuck the conference materials. "I think it would be valuable to hear someone with a different perspective on the implications of aging in America. And frankly, I think Henry Fenwick would also benefit by attending with me." I threw in Henry, editor-in-chief of *Modern Maturity*, to make it all seem less self-serving.

Chuck looked at the materials, then at me, then at the materials again. Knowing what a political animal he was, I figured he was trying to divine what management would want him to do.

When he finally spoke, his friendly tone surprised me, as did his answer. "All right, I'll submit your request."

A few days later, Henry and I got permission to fly to San Francisco and attend the conference. I had pulled it off. And Henry, a witty and intellectual Brit, would be the perfect traveling companion.

I was excited about the opportunity to meet Dychtwald, the author of *Age Wave*, the book that had changed my thinking about aging. His premise—that many of us would live longer, healthier lives than expected and therefore we should prepare for it—had inspired me. It had especially resonated with me after my encounter with the brutally ageist headhunter in New York.

The conference, held at the Nikko Hotel, began with Dychtwald's riveting presentation. He surprised me with his theatrics as he pranced back and forth across the stage like an evangelist. Such motivational speakers are more common today.

Using an enormous screen, he showed us slides of American society in the fifties, sixties, seventies, and eighties. He dramatized the demographic changes that have occurred since World War II, beginning with the baby boom, and highlighted the societal implications.

His childlike enthusiasm was infectious, if somewhat over-the-top. To my ear, his was a welcome new voice that sounded distinctly like a call to arms.

According to Dychtwald, "We will live much longer than you might expect, and with the help of science and medicine many will experience no disease and little decline. Therefore, we must retire the myths that define aging as a period of decay. Only then will we fulfill our human potential."

I liked that message. It spoke to me directly.

As the conference was ending for the day, I approached Dychtwald and introduced myself. A ruggedly handsome, animated man, Dychtwald was in stark contrast to the bland organization types of AARP.

"Ken, I can't tell you how inspired I was by your presentation," I gushed. "I hope your hopes for the future come true and that we can all look forward to a richly rewarding longevity. In order to reap the benefits, though, we have to educate the public about taking responsibility for their own well being. Otherwise we will just have sick people living longer."

Ken's eyes brightened. "Ah, as Shakespeare said, 'There's the rub.'"

As we talked, I felt an almost instant rapport with the man. But it was over all too soon. As we shook hands good-bye, he smiled and said, "If you ever get tired of AARP, call me." And then he was gone.

That invitation stayed with me as I flew back to New York. Looking out the window as the vast landscape quickly passed below, I realized I was bone-weary of AARP. I couldn't imagine spending another year, much less the rest of my working life, in that stultifying environment. Ken's philosophy of renewal and reinvention roiled through my mind.

I had just received an invitation, sort of, to live in California. It would give me the opportunity to fulfill my lifelong fantasy of settling in Sausalito, the seaside town just north of the Golden Gate Bridge. I'd fallen in love with it during that business trip years ago.

Back in New York, I waited a few days and then made the call. "Hello, Ken," I said in my cheeriest voice. "I've been thinking a lot about your invitation to call if I ever got tired of AARP. Your timing was perfect, because I'm feeling the need for a new challenge."

"Great timing at my end, too, Leda. My wife, Maddy, and I are going to be in New York in two weeks. Let's meet at the Waldorf and kick this around."

In October I met with Ken and Maddy, who looked svelte and glamorous in a clingy Donna Karen black dress. Her warm smile put me at ease from the start. Together they projected the aura of a Hollywood star couple.

Ken filled me in on the genesis of *Age Wave,* which I already knew since I had read his book and reread it on the plane coming back from California.

"As you know, Leda, I am a product of the human-potential movement and a strong proponent of it. I came to California in 1973 to live and teach at the Esalen Institute in Big Sur. My primary interest at that time was researching strategies and techniques by which people could enhance their creativity, physical vigor, and mental capacities. Through this work I met a most extraordinary woman, Dr. Gay Luce, who was planning a grand experiment, a kind of academy of holistic health and human development. She was looking for someone to work with her. That's what led to me working with people over sixty-five, my introduction to gerontology. I never expected to spend most of my life searching for a new paradigm of aging in America. If you've read my book, you know all this."

I listened intently, though it was all familiar. It was evident that day and for years to follow that Ken never tired of telling his own story. After all, his success depended greatly on an outsized ego. As he continued, his enthusiasm for Age Wave escalated.

"Age Wave today is a company that specializes in research, consulting, forecasting, and presentations for corporations interested in understanding the mature population. We show corporations how to prepare for the coming age wave and thus capitalize on its opportunities."

He finally took a breath, so I squeezed in. "I'm eager to hear more, Ken."

"Leda, first tell me about yourself and how you ended up at AARP."

"Well, it's a long story. As you saw in the résumé I sent you—a rather unorthodox one—I've worked at every level of the publishing business. But my true love is creating new things."

"But as advertising director, your primary responsibility was selling, right?" Ken sat forward in his chair.

I took the cue and began to talk about my sales connections and achievements, his obvious interest. "I know key decision makers in advertising, and I can reach the executives who control the ad budgets." I took a deep breath and asked, "So, how do you see me fitting into Age Wave?"

Ken stood and walked to the window of his Waldorf suite. Looking out at the busy Manhattan streets, he said, "Leda, we want to start a publishing company that will specialize in books and magazines that reach the fifty-plus audience. We've just hired the president for this new division of Age Wave, and I was hoping, if we can get together, you wouldn't mind taking a lesser title. If you're at all interested, can you visit our offices in Emeryville, across the bay from San Francisco?"

I tried to contain my excitement at the idea of involvement in a publishing start-up. "Well, I'm scheduled to go to Fort Lauderdale to spend Christmas with my sister and her family. Why don't I fly to California from there on New Year's Day?"

"Terrific," Ken replied with genuine enthusiasm. "What a cool way to start the New Year."

* * *

Back in New York, I shared this life-changing possibility with my close friends, my family, and Peter. Their reaction was unanimous.

"Are you crazy? At your age you're going to start over in California? Leave a secure job with a solid organization? Give up your rent-controlled apartment, your friends, Manhattan, and take a chance that you'll like living in Sausalito? Those people are hippies. They wear Birkenstocks. And do you know how far California is from Europe?"

I knew their objections were valid. But I also knew this might be my last chance to realize my Sausalito dream.

Peter was aghast. "Why would you do this?" he kept saying. The idea of not lunching regularly at Le Cirque was incomprehensible. As was the idea of anyone of sound mind wanting to live outside Manhattan.

But I had grown bored of the repetitive fancy lunches and dinners, the same faces sitting at the same tables at the same restaurants. I was craving less steel and concrete, more nature and greenery—a place where flowers bloomed year round. Sausalito reminded me of the Italian Riviera, while the nearby Marin Headlands, a national park, resembled the Irish countryside. That I was six thousand miles from Europe wouldn't matter.

On the other hand, moving to the west coast could mean the end of Peter and me. My girlfriends, many of them unmarried and at least ten years younger, focused on that loss.

"Isn't there a risk in leaving him?" they asked over and over. "A good man is hard to find."

"Perhaps," I'd reply coolly. "But that's a chance I'll have to take."

Fact is, Peter and I didn't have that much in common apart from sex. We weren't anything near soul mates. We got along well because we could talk business and shared a real passion for the many facets of publishing and printing. But his inability to comprehend my desire to move west exposed and then widened the gap between us. Maybe that explains why I never felt jealous around Peter. Of course, I knew he wasn't loyal. He managed to maintain a reputation as a loving father and husband while openly courting women in New York restaurants. I accepted that. I didn't want a soap-opera romance; I'd already had a lifetime of drama with Mort.

Could I depend on Peter if my move to California failed? No, I didn't think so. I had to depend on myself.

Ignoring the prophecies of doom from friends and family, I flew to San Francisco to visit the Age Wave offices. Emeryville offered a stunning view of San Francisco, which looked like an island buffeted by waves of fog.

I spent the day touring the offices and meeting the entire staff. A few ex-New Yorkers welcomed me like an old friend. A common bond links all New Yorkers, as though we've gone into battle together.

I had lunch with Michael Rybarski, newly appointed president of the publishing division. I knew if he didn't like me, this dream would go poof like a soap bubble. Fortunately we hit if off. Michael was an enthusiastic intellectual with charm.

The next day Ken bounded up to me. "Well, what do you think?"

"Ken, you have a lot of eggheads here," I responded incautiously.

He knew what I meant—he had an army of thinkers, most of them lacking street experience.

"You're right," he shot back. "We need someone like you who's been in the trenches and knows the marketplace."

I nodded—trenches indeed.

"Since we already have a president, your title would be vice president of custom publishing. Now, what else can I tell you?"

"Make me an offer, Ken."

He was startled by my boldness, but it reinforced his belief that I could close a sale. "That's it? Well, okay. I'll have an offer and agreement drawn up and ready for you to review in the morning."

Ken went on. "If it's acceptable, Maddy will help you look for a place to live. Until then you can stay at the Claremont Hotel. I suppose you'll eventually want to live in San Francisco?"

"Oh, no, Ken. I want to live in Sausalito."

Ken's eyebrows shot up. "Are you sure? Have you thought it through? Most of us here at Age Wave live in the East Bay suburbs. Do you know what it's like over there? It's scenic all right, but it has a weird mix of hippy types, refugees from the sixties."

I wanted that Sausalito view, the one that reminded me of Italy. I'd find out later if I could accept the culture. "*Very* sure," I answered emphatically.

The next day Ken presented me with a one-year contract that defined his offer: a six-figure salary, generous travel expenses, and because I'd said I intended to keep my New York apartment, the right to stay there whenever in New York on business and to charge meals and a per diem to the company.

"I accept."

"Done," Ken said happily.

We exchanged smiles and shook hands.

The following day, accompanied by Maddy and a realtor, I explored the Sausalito apartment scene. As we drove to Marin County, they both tried to persuade me that I would prefer Mill Valley, a lovely village in the shadow of Mt. Tamalpais; or maybe Tiburon, a more polished seaside town. I declined.

On that cold and rainy day, the realtor took me to the Cote d'Azur condominiums situated at the bottom of Alexander Avenue, the road that winds down from the Golden Gate Bridge into Sausalito. We walked through the front door of the unit, and I headed straight for the balcony that overlooked Angel Island. It was the view I had first seen and fallen in love with years ago.

"It's seventeen hundred a month, unfurnished and available immediately," the realtor offered.

"I'll take it," I said without hesitation. "It's perfect."

"Well, you do make fast decisions."

"So I'm told."

My resignation from AARP met no resistance. For Chuck it was probably the fulfillment of a wish. I was a thorn in his side and a challenge to his management capabilities. *Good-bye and good riddance,* he probably thought.

16. Get up and Go

When I moved to my two-bedroom condo in Sausalito, I shopped for what I call "throwaway furniture." If I didn't like living there, I would simply throw or give it all away and go back to my beautifully furnished home in New York. I was neither naïve nor impetuous enough to give that up. It was my security blanket.

But so far, life in Sausalito was going my way. Each morning I awakened before sunrise and took a walk downhill into the heart of Sausalito. Starbucks was just opening, and sometimes I was the first one in the door. I'd take my dry cappuccino to the counter by the window and watch the day lighten, all the while saying a prayer of thanks. The window faced the San Francisco skyline, which gradually appeared across the bay through the morning mist.

My fantasy had come true. I had always dreamed of living alone in this natural paradise, and now I was doing it: blissfully alone by the sea in Sausalito.

* * *

On my first day on the job, the staff was called to the conference room to welcome me. Following those pleasantries, Michael Rybarksi unveiled a complex chart illustrating key events in our lives including marriage, childbirth, divorce, loss of parent, and children going to college. He argued that although such milestones couldn't always be linked to a specific age, they did impact consumer behavior. The theory became a useful tool to help us develop marketing strategies based on life stage rather than age. It sure beat making broad assumptions about people based solely on their age, which was the norm of the time.

It occurred to me that I was by far the oldest person in the room and had lived through most of the key events the chart covered.

"Which segment offers the greatest opportunity for a marketer?" Michael asked the group.

"That's easy," I boldly interjected. "Single women who are divorced or widowed and over fifty—that's the fastest growing demographic. I can identify with them since I am one. And after working at AARP, I can confirm that almost nothing is being done to reach this group. Most advertisers don't even consider older women because they're convinced they aren't a lucrative market."

Michael beamed, as though I'd just hit a jackpot on the dollar-slots. "That's it! First we develop a custom publication that targets this group, then we identify the advertisers with big budgets. Leda, who do you know that fits this description?"

"Well, off the top of my head, Phil Guarascio, advertising director for General Motors. He controls the biggest ad budget in the world—and I can get to him. He's open to new ideas and very gutsy. He knows me and has always supported my ventures."

"Go for it," Michael said, pumping his fist. Then he said to the group, in the manner of a halftime football coach: "Okay, team, let's go!"

* * *

Over the next two months, we ran focus groups with women over fifty. While capturing information on their needs and interests, we measured their preferences for magazine titles. The winner—*Get Up & Go! The magazine for women living anew*—was the hands-down favorite.

I enjoyed this phase of the job, enjoyed delving into the minds of people whom nobody was talking to. The focus groups revealed vast unmet needs. Clearly, advertisers could reap huge financial rewards.

It was my job to produce the bimonthly mini-magazine *Get Up & Go!* and to connect with readers so intimately that they'd trust our advertisers enough to buy their products.

Armed with reams of research and a presentation for *Get Up & Go!*, Michael and I flew to Detroit to meet with Phil Guarascio at General

Motors. We needed to sell the project to him if it was going to become a reality.

We were shown to the GM conference room, and soon Phil appeared with an associate. After introductions, he sat down, put his feet up on the conference table, and said, "Okay, what do you have to show me?"

While Michael set up the projection equipment, Phil stared at me with a look that said, "This better be good."

"Phil, we're here to blow you away with a fully integrated marketing program that will deliver measurable results," said Michael, his face ruddy with excitement. "Based on our work with the fifty-plus population, we now know that one of the most neglected segments is divorced and widowed women. More and more they are making car-buying decisions, but they're uncomfortable with car dealers. Even afraid."

As Michael continued, I realized what a dynamic and persuasive speaker he was. He really could sell ice to Eskimos, and I was pleased to be his partner.

"Our program is designed to build a relationship with these women and foster trust via a free magazine mailed to their homes. It's designed to literally drive them to the car dealer to make a purchase. With our database, we can locate and reach the ready-to-buy customer."

Michael was on a roll, commanding our attention.

"In conjunction with our magazine, we will create a dealer newsletter that educates dealers and their salespeople on how to connect with these women."

As Michael finished his presentation, I looked at Phil for clues—was he buying? Before I could decide, he turned to his associate and said, "This is perfect for Buick. Inform Denny about it."

Turning back to us, he declared, "I'm willing to finance a test of this. I will give you ten grand to develop the mini-magazine you described. Come back in a month and show me the product." Then he flashed me a grin and added, "If Leda is the editor, I'm sure it'll be interesting."

What a pal, I thought, *complimenting me in front of my boss.*

Michael and I fairly skipped through the lobby and out onto Grand Avenue.

"Okay, Michael, that ten thousand is mine! Mine to develop the product." I wanted clarity on that point, lest he think he could appropriate some for other areas—say, for more charts and graphs.

117

Emboldened, I added, "And I want complete control over the execution of *Get Up & Go!* I want to use Paul Hardy, my art director in New York."

"New York?" Michael stammered. "Why can't Jackie do it? Or some art director in the Bay Area?"

"Sorry, Michael. This is a great concept, and it's going to require a great talent to understand it and execute it. That's Paul."

"Ken is not going to like this, Leda. He wants people to be on the premises."

That annoyed me. "Why? So he can stand over the designer's shoulder and meddle?"

"How can you work with someone three thousand miles away?" he persisted.

"He's not three thousand miles away. We are. We're three thousand miles away from the creative heart of America. Paul can do this, in spite of the distance, because he has the talent required and the sensibilities necessary to understand my editorial direction. Besides, we have computers."

What could Michael say? I had the client connection and thus the upper hand.

* * *

Paul and I developed the prototype for *Get Up & Go! The magazine for women living anew* on the dining room table in my New York apartment with the help of Valorie Weaver, another New York creative colleague who had developed *Self* magazine. Prototype in hand, we flew to Detroit to meet Phil. We pitched a complex marketing strategy that would serve as a test. We recommended testing the program in Florida and Illinois, two states with plenty of people who fit the desired profile: single women of a certain age who owned cars in need of replacement.

Phil was impressed, and Buick bought the program. For the next three years, I enjoyed not only the financial rewards of the deal, but the satisfaction of having created a truly original and effective product that helped single women.

Get Up & Go! was a success for advertisers and publishers alike. It helped launch other ground-breaking Age Wave publications targeting specific demographic groups, such as retired couples or busy parents.

* * *

After three years I decided to give up my New York apartment, downscale my possessions, and buy a condo in the building where I lived. I knew I would never go back to New York.

What I didn't know was that my sons would follow me out west. Roughly three years after I left New York for good, Scott and his wife, Annette, moved to San Francisco. Three years later, Robert and his cat, Marilyn, followed. They settled in Sausalito. Having my sons nearby was a blessing I hadn't counted on when I left New York.

I continued to see Peter when I was in New York, but best of all were our long-distance phone calls. Typically, he got home to his New York *pied à terre* about eleven New York time, just as I was finishing dinner in California. We would then enjoy a phone intimacy that was intense.

I liked the bicoastal arrangement, and I think Peter did too. His wife was dying of cancer and he needed a friend, which I tried to be. Peter was more vulnerable now, and I was more sensitive to his pain, so our relationship deepened.

* * *

Riding the success of *Get Up & Go!*, Ken and his associates set about expanding the influence and profit potential of Age Wave. Brought on board were new people with exaggerated expectations for the Age Wave brand. Venture capital was readily available in the nineties, and the new management was extending its tentacles to reach anyone with a checkbook.

Age Wave pursued a breathless expansion, which included a chain of home-healthcare superstores and Lifesource Nutrition Solutions, a company specializing in home-delivered food nutritionally tailored to the dietary needs of older adults.

Meanwhile, as it turned out, *Get Up & Go!* wasn't all that profitable— at least not profitable enough for the venture capitalists. As a result, my original magazine concept was transformed into a national chain of free senior newspapers. The focus was no longer just on women.

I became the supervising editor of thirty-six regional newspapers. With dozens of ego-bloated editors reporting to me, the complexity of coordinating it all challenged my expertise. Putting humility aside, I believe the newspapers were very good. Paul Hardy's eye-catching design once again showcased his unique talent. Yet I never felt that Ken fully appreciated our accomplishments or hard work.

It was a high-stress job, but I was having fun. That is, until Ken hired some Wall Street types, whose main contribution was to look like successful Wall Street types. Ken also opened offices on Wall Street, befitting his new kingdom. They were not open for long.

The walls came tumbling down in 2000. When the Internet bubble burst, venture capital dried up everywhere. We crashed with a thud. Everyone was terminated, and the stock options that had helped motivate us, that represented our nest eggs, evaporated. I was left with nothing but memories to show for the eight years I'd invested in the company.

Was I bitter? Angry? Yes, indeed. I was discharged with the rest of the staff, given no special treatment for having changed my life so dramatically to join Age Wave. My Age Wave stock was now worthless, and I received no other compensation.

It was Michael who broke the news to me. It was so traumatic I barely remember his words. Nor do I remember much of the end. After everyone left, I stayed for a few days, leisurely gathering and sorting my files, concrete evidence of eight years of good work. Now, almost a decade later, it gives me pleasure to review that work and much satisfaction to see its enduring relevance.

* * *

My life in California was in jeopardy. What to do? Before I could even think about looking for work, I began to receive calls from prospective employers. One was from Kellene Giloff, who wanted me to join her company, Stampington. She wanted to start a magazine for older women called *Ageless*.

"I was told you're an expert on mature women," she said.

"Yes, I think I am," I replied.

"I'd love to meet and talk."

I agreed to help her develop and launch the magazine. It was fun while it lasted—three issues, as I'd silently predicted. It was the same old problem: lagging circulation and investor impatience. They simply wouldn't allow enough time for the publication to find an audience or to prove to advertisers that it had one.

Working as an independent contractor, I did some consulting work before establishing a prized connection with American Express Custom publishing, where I worked for three years. An added bonus: several trips to New York, where I visited with old friends and had an occasional tryst with Peter.

"Have you had enough of California?" he asked me one evening, not for the first time. We were having drinks at the Plaza. "Are you ready to come back to the real world?"

"No, Peter," I replied. "I love New York and really enjoy sharing the best of it with you. But it's really a case of been there, done that. I wish I could seduce you with the natural beauty surrounding me in the Bay Area. How the air sparkles on a clear day. You can practically taste the freshness. I gulp it in on my walks every morning and at the Marin Headlands. I now understand why my father had to go back to Tuscany and probably why he lived to be ninety-two."

Peter looked at me quizzically, and I knew we were speaking different languages. It didn't stop me. "I want to be alive—I mean alive and healthy—for a long time. I have a better chance of that in Sausalito than here. New York is not a good place to grow old—unless you're rich."

17. THE THIRD AGE

Consulting kept me alive financially, but living in Sausalito nourished my heart, soul, and body. Thanks to walks in the countryside and fresh foods from the farmers market, I never felt healthier. I slept well too, becalmed by the view through my bedroom window: the moon rising over Angel Island.

I had made new female friends, most of them at least ten years younger—adventurous women who were excellent walking partners, fun to talk to, and game for anything. Together we explored magnificent Marin and the adjacent areas, from Carmel to Napa. It was all new to me. When I suggested we go take mud baths in Calistoga, a favorite experience of mine but foreign and somewhat creepy to my friends, they acceded and off we went. Once initiated, they became aficionados like me, and the baths became a regular part of our drives to Napa.

The men I met were less interesting. Conversation revolved around their toys, from bicycles to boats, and sports the California climate is so suited to: sailing, cycling, and hiking. They were usually dressed for those activities. Most had been to Hawaii but not to Europe. *Stark contrast,* I thought, *to the sartorial peacocks like Phil Guarascio and Peter Faucetta with their custom-made suits and Italian shoes,* de rigueur *in the watering holes they frequented.*

Meanwhile, on the work front, I pitched myself as the grand dame of the mature market and was able to attract consulting work and continue to support my lifestyle.

In 2000, my first grandchild, Miles, burst into my life like a shooting star.

I'd never really thought about being a grandmother, and ecstasy was not my first emotion when he arrived. No, that evolved as I spent more time with the little boy who eventually took center stage in my life. I was not alone in responding to Miles's unique personality. More than one friend, charmed by his sweet sociability, remarked that he was an old soul. I'd never heard this expression before, but I liked it.

As Miles and I talked and played together, we forged a connection I never thought possible with a child. We spent many an afternoon sharing milk and cookies. When I sang a little Italian ditty about a mouse climbing up a tree and then tumbling down, he always erupted into peals of laughter, and I did too.

Once my sons were grown, children had ceased to be a source of interest or delight for me. I saw them as annoying, disruptive of my career. Now my grandchildren have become my chief passion.

A few months after Miles entered the world, my father left it.

Fausto Giovannetti died at age ninety-two in his beloved home in Pievefosciana, Italy. Because of professional commitments, neither my sister nor I were with him when he passed away. A good friend and his housekeeper, who'd been with him for years, were by his side at the end.

His whole life, Fausto had harshly criticized the Catholic Church. He was a typical Italian anticlerical—that is, he believed that Jesus was the son of God and that Christianity was the one true faith but that the church had become hopelessly corrupt. "It's in the interest of the church to keep the masses ignorant and condemn them to propagating more children to increase their numbers," he would say or, "The church's teachings have nothing to do with the teachings of Jesus Christ."

* * *

After Fausto died, Paola and I traveled to Italy to settle property issues and to review his belongings.

Not surprisingly, he made his last wishes clear: no priest was to come near him. His body was to be cremated, something frowned upon in Italy and difficult to accomplish. Cremation is allowed only in licensed locations, and the bureaucratic red tape is daunting, expensive, and time consuming, like many things in Italy. It's also against the law to scatter ashes, and that prevented us from fulfilling Fausto's last wish: to have his ashes strewn over the Tuscan hills near his house. Although I was willing to break the law, my sister was uncomfortable with the idea of getting involved with the Italian authorities.

My father's remains were sent to Pisa to be cremated, and then his ashes were returned to Pievefosciana, where they were placed in a hillside cemetery.

My sister and I were the only beneficiaries of his estate—his house and its contents.

As we sorted through his self-published books, his paintings of flowers, fruit, and the Italian landscape he so loved, we reminisced and laughed, sharing a closeness we'd never known before. We were kids again, reliving that year we'd spent together in Italy. I was fifteen, Paola was eleven. We recalled walks in the countryside, gathering chestnuts from the fields, and placing fresh flowers at the little roadside shrines that dot the country roads.

It took us a week to sort through Fausto's belongings and empty the house. We sold the place to the housekeeper and split the proceeds. We burned the things we didn't want, including his collection of every magazine I had worked on. They had been neatly stored in the basement.

We found nothing of value. Paola took a few of his inventions, gizmos that looked like museum pieces. I took some of the books he'd written (common subjects were how much he loved his birthplace, Pieve, and his disillusionment with Fascism), a few paintings, and some heavy antique Italian linens.

Then we closed the shutters on Fausto's house for the last time.

As we walked away, I thought, *He never really knew us. Worse than that, he never loved us.* Although Paola and I never spoke of this, I was sure she felt it too. The belief that your father never loved you is like a wound that never heals no matter what you do to compensate for the absence of that love. For Paola, material possessions filled the void. For me, achievement, recognition, and romantic adventures forged my identity as a strong and independent woman.

* * *

As we age, it's important to feel we've done everything we wanted. Even though I've made mistakes and suffered setbacks, I bounced back, recovered, and renewed myself.

Europeans call old age the Third Age.

In this final stage of my life, I can enjoy my memories. I try to siphon positive energy from them. Mistakes or not, I have no regrets. Not my days spent as a dedicated housewife, nor my years jet-setting around the world doing stimulating work and having illicit love affairs. And certainly not falling in love with my grandchildren. No, no regrets.

* * *

A collection of the essays I wrote in my column for *Get Up & Go!* were published in 2006. The book, called *Look for the Moon in the Morning*, encourages older women to make the most of their golden years. Its publication brought me much satisfaction and pride. I started giving talks to women's groups, where I often retell the story of my firing from *Bon Appétit* and how I overcame that and other setbacks.

I intend to continue encouraging women to assess their personal resources and focus on making good decisions. Reinvention at any age takes guts, but it is never impossible.

It just requires pure moxie.

Breinigsville, PA USA
12 November 2010
249212BV00001B/6/P